20

To Bob Brent,

with affection and

admiration —

from "the genius"

Mar[illegible]

From a Single Window

From a Single Window

Michigan State University and Its Press, 1947–1997

Maurice Hungiville

Michigan State University Press
East Lansing

All Michigan State University Press Books are produced on paper which meets the requirements of American National Standard of Information Sciences—Permanence of paper for printed materials ANSI Z23.48–1984

Printed in the United States of America

Michigan State University Press

East Lansing, Michigan 48823–5202

06 05 04 03 02 01 00 99 98   1 2 3 4 5 6 7 8 9 10

LIBRARY OF CONGRESS CATALOGING-IN-PUBLICATION DATA

Maurice Hungiville: From A Single Window: Michigan State University and its Press, 1947-1997/Maurice Hungiville

    p.   cm.

    Includes bibliographical references and index (p.).

    ISBN 0870134299 (alk. paper)

    Z473.M598 H86 1997 070.5/94/0977427 21

    Michigan State University Press – History. University presses—United States—History—20th century. University presses—Michigan—East Lansing – History—20th century. Scholarly publishing—United States—History—20th century. Scholarly publishing—Michigan—East Lansing—History—20th century. Michigan State University Press.Control No.: 97034994

To Rita Stevenson

"This isn't just an epigram—life is much more successfully looked at from a single window, after all."

F. Scott Fitzgerald
The Great Gatsby

CONTENTS

Preface ix

Chapter 1 A Separate Institution 1

Chapter 2 "An Interesting Fellow" 23

Chapter 3 A One Man Operation 55

Chapter 4 Out of Fashion 71

Chapter 5 A Holding Operation 83

Chapter 6 To Revitalize the Press 93

Chapter 7 Chapin's Challenge 103

Chapter 8 Doubletake: The Historian as Publisher 111

Chapter 9 From This Single Window 133

Endnotes 135

Bibliography 139

Index 143

PREFACE

Most American organizations suffer from a kind of Alzheimer's disease: they are without institutional memory. "Those who are ignorant of the past," as George Santayana has warned, "are doomed to repeat it." If Santayana is right, Michigan State University could do worse—much worse—than repeat the past between the years 1954 and 1969, its "golden years," when Lyle Blair's press was the only department in the university as famous as the football team. While the nation's sports pages celebrated the victories of Biggie Munn and Duffy Daugherty, the literary pages of the *New York Times*, the *Saturday Review*, and the *New York Review of Books* celebrated Lyle Blair's books.

P. F. Kluge makes a fine point in *Alma Mater*, his splendid history of Kenyon College. Kenyon's English department in the early 1940s included faculty members such as John Crowe Ransom, who attracted students such as Peter Taylor, Randall Jarrell, and Robert Lowell. There are, Kluge noted, two things you can do with reputations: you can live off them or you can live up to them.[1] In the 1970s Michigan State University chose to live off the reputation of its distinguished press and ultimately to neglect and almost forget it. This history, then, is a reminder, literally an attempt to re-mind or re-instate in the collective mind of the university, the memory of a once remarkable, then endangered, press. That press over the years was almost destroyed, but eventually rescued and renewed. This volume celebrates its fiftieth anniversary.

There are only a few histories of American university presses. Some of these take the form of memoirs written by retired press directors. August Frugé's *A Skeptic among Scholars* is a lively, insightful example of this genre. Max Hall's *Harvard University Press* is a fine traditional history complete with bibliography. There should be more, a lot more, histories because there is much to be learned from university presses. They are, among other things, unexploited archives, repositories of unexamined correspondence and valuable biographical data.

Life, as F. Scott Fitzgerald's Nick Carraway observed, can best be seen from a single window. From the window of MSU's university press can be seen something of the larger history of the university and the powerful forces that formed—and sometimes deformed—it over an exciting span of fifty years. The huge growth of enrollment stimulated by the G. I. Bill after World War II, the ferocious anti-Communism of the 1950s, the student protests of the 1960s and early 1970s, and the inflation and recessions of the late 1970s and 1980s all touched the Press.

Unless otherwise noted, all quotations are from documents in the Michigan State University Press archives maintained in the Manly Miles Building. Each author's file contains correspondence and book reviews. Minutes of Board of Directors meetings are in bound volumes. The five Michigan State University Press directors share a common concern for history. Without their careful maintenance of records, this book would not have been possible.

In order to minimize the notes that usually document and—all too often—disfigure scholarly prose, the correspondence, memoranda, minutes of meetings, and book reviews used to research this book will not be cited. Photocopies of all materials quoted in the text will be maintained in a Press history file in the archive.

To the Press's present director, Fred C. Bohm, and his staff I owe a special acknowledgment. The idea for this admiring but by no means reverential history was his. When Bohm learned that I was at work on a biography of Russel Nye, MSU's only Pulitzer Prize-winning professor, he asked me to write an introduction to a new, paperback edition of Nye's and Martin Gardner's classic, *The Wizard of Oz and Who He Was*, which he was about to publish. After the project was completed he suggested that I write the text for a brief brochure to celebrate Michigan State University Press's fiftieth anniversary. Thanks to the work of its five directors—James Denison, Lyle Blair, Jean Busfield, Richard Chapin, and Fred Bohm—I have been able to write a bit more than a birthday card.

I must also acknowledge those who lent their eyes and ears and minds to this history. Wilma Miller lent her ears to the task of transcribing Lyle Blair's 1985 tape-recorded comments on the Press. Erin McNitt's young vision gave me access to the faded pages of MSU's student newspaper. Ryan Stevenson and Jesse Howard gave patient remedial instruction concerning computers. Bill Range, an admired former student, did some heavy lifting, and Steve Thelander made his personal library available to me. Dorothy Frye and Stacy Gould helped locate documents and photographs in the Michigan State University Archives. Anne Ginther and

Beverly Weber of the Media Communications Office, and Maurice Crane of the Michigan State University Voice Library helped me learn about MSU history. Rita Stevenson and Carol Parker, as always, encouraged and inspired.

To some it might seem premature—if not pretentious—to offer a history of Michigan State University Press after only fifty years. Yet its founders published a history in 1950, after only three short years of life. For that small booklet, *The Michigan State College Press: Guidelines to its History and Objectives,*[2] I am grateful; let's hope that those who write the centennial history of the Press in 2047 will be grateful for this effort.

Maurice Hungiville
East Lansing
May 1998

Chapter 1

A SEPARATE INSTITUTION

American university presses are a part of the British scholarly publishing heritage transplanted in American soil. Oxford University Press (founded in 1478) and Cambridge University Press (founded in 1537) were established at a time when they could exploit the new technology of moveable type. As time passed, British scholarly publishers had the advantage of profitable backlists nurtured for centuries. The Bible and *The Book of Common Prayer* were perennial bestsellers that helped finance monumental projects like the *Cambridge Modern History* and The *Oxford English Dictionary*, which required some seventy years of scholarly labor.[1]

Seeing the close connection between intellectual inquiry within the university and scholarly publishing that had been firmly established by their predecessors across the Atlantic, the founders of many of America's great universities also became the founders of the nation's first university presses. Daniel Coit Gilman of Johns Hopkins University, William Rainey Harper of the University of Chicago, and Nicolas Murray Butler of Columbia all founded presses a few years after they had established their institutions of higher learning. Scholarly publishing was, to each of them, central to the idea of a university. Gilman, who founded Johns Hopkins in 1878, offered one of the first—and best—justifications for a university press. "It is," he said, "one of the noblest duties of a university to advance knowledge, and to diffuse it not merely among those who can attend the daily lectures—but far and wide."[2]

Michigan State University Press's origins, however, are not shrouded in any such sense of noble duty. Instead, they were derived from an odd mixture of motives, a combination of frustration and ambition. The frustration came from members of the college's bookstore committee; the ambition came from its twelfth president, John A. Hannah.

Born in Grand Rapids, Michigan, in 1902, Hannah had been president of Michigan State College for only six years in 1947. His educational background was modest. He had only one undergraduate degree from the school he now led, and that degree was in the unpretentious field of poultry science.

His background may have seemed limited, but his ambitions for this small college of 13,282 students were not. In 1947, the year he founded the Press, he also hired a new football coach, Clarence "Biggie" Munn, from Syracuse University. Both decisions would eventually bring national recognition to Michigan State.

LAYING THE GROUNDWORK

In early 1947, members of the MSC Bookstore Committee had become frustrated by their having to deal with the perennial problem of printing textbooks and other course materials. In a one-page memo to President Hannah, committee chair E. G. Foster passed along a unanimously adopted committee resolution asking that "the bookstore be relieved of the function and risk of printing material prepared by the staff and that a separate organization be established to undertake these activities. . . ." Those who sold the books were clearly tired of printing them, and the Bookstore Committee, after urging that another committee be appointed to study their proposal, listed the possible benefits: "Establishment of a College Press would have definite prestige value," and "staff members might be encouraged to do more and better writing." The memo found a receptive audience in the president's office.

John Hannah, as David Murley has pointed out in an unpublished M. A. thesis, was steadfast in defending his faculty members' constitutional rights from anti-Communist assaults. Other college presidents, most with educations that were more extensive and in possession of degrees from elite institutions, often caved in under political pressures and simply fired scholars whose loyalties were questioned; in some cases they even imposed loyalty oaths on every faculty member. Likewise, Hannah's record with regard to scholarly publishing was considerably more enlightened and notably more supportive than those of some of his peers whose formal credentials appeared to be more impressive.[3]

In 1943—just four years before Hannah started Michigan State's press—Harvard University's president, James B. Conant, tried to eliminate his institution's sadly neglected seventy-one-year-old scholarly publishing operation. He told its director, the distinguished biographer of Thomas Jefferson, Dumas Malone, that he was not satisfied with Harvard University Press as a business enterprise. Astonished to learn that he was expected to be an entrepreneur, Malone promptly resigned.

Michigan State University president John A. Hannah

His letter of resignation, dated 17 July 1943, expressed his refusal to remain in a position "where the major criteria by which my work is judged differ materially from those applied to the academic departments of the university."[4]

In the midst of this crisis, a Harvard professor who had won a Pulitzer Prize for his biography of William James offered an eloquent and pragmatic defense of both academic publishing and scholarship. A university, Ralph Barton Perry explained,

> holds in its hands and can apply a seal of scholarly honesty and accuracy. Its name is a certificate of quality. In their capacity as scholars, its members write not what they think they can sell, but the conclusions they have reached as a result of thorough and expert inquiry. They are not obliged to cater to appetites and purchasing power. The public, therefore, has confidence in the university's disinterestedness and good faith.[5]

Harvard's President Conant, a distinguished scientist preoccupied with service to the nation during World War II, never arrived at an understanding of scholarly publishing. Even after Professor Perry's eloquent explanation and Dumas Malone's potentially instructive resignation, Conant wrote: "Much as I feel if we were honest and brave, we would give up the Press, we cannot undertake the gruesome slaughter. The death agonies would drag out for many years because of the nature of our contracts and many commitments." If left to himself, Conant confessed, he "might well be the executioner of Harvard University Press."[6]

John Hannah's attitude about a proposed press at Michigan State College was more enlightened. His values, ironically, were larger, more open than his formal education might suggest. His idea of a university included a scholarly press.

JOHN HANNAH APPOINTS A PRESS DIRECTOR

Hannah's desire to create a Michigan State College Press may also have had something to do with his own interest in "more and better writing." A month before he read the Bookstore Committee's memo, he hired James H. Denison as an administrative assistant. Denison, who had been a reporter for the *Detroit Free Press* and a speech writer for Michigan Governor Harry Kelly, was hired for his writing ability. He became, among a great many other things, an administrative writer-in-residence responsible for the flow of words out of the president's office. Years later, Denison would recall the many times a staff member would seek Hannah's signature on a garbled, needlessly complex letter. Hannah would hand the document to Denison and say, "make this sound like me," or, "put this in English."

It was to a journalist, then, that John Hannah turned when he wanted to start a press. Denison could write and act, edit a turgid letter, and organize complex projects. Over the years, until his retirement in 1969, he would perform a variety of tasks for the president. In 1954, for instance, he was one of four people Hannah chose to send to Saigon to initiate what would become Michigan State University's frustrating experience in "nation building." On campus, Denison's less dramatic duties included directing public relations; administering the college radio station, WKAR; and, of course, writing speeches. Over the years he would draft 51 major addresses and 334 "presentations" for Hannah. Above all, he transformed the vague idea of a college press into a concrete institution.

On 16 April 1947—nineteen days after the Bookstore Committee's complaint—Denison was named chairman of the committee created to study possibilities for giving relief to the bookstore. The Denison committee recommended establishing the Michigan State College Press with a $50,000 fund transfer, which would be repaid from anticipated profits. By 19 June the Denison committee's recommendations had been approved by President Hannah, the faculty, and the State Board of Agriculture, and James Denison, the forty-year-old administrative assistant, was appointed director of Michigan State College Press.

Two years later, on 23 June 1949, the small, newly organized Press was transformed from a Michigan State College "department" into a not-for-profit corporation. The incorporators, John Hannah, Clark McDonel, and Philip May, promptly elected Hannah chairman and signed the articles of incorporation. Seven days later they adopted bylaws calling for a Board of Directors consisting of ten members. The college's president would appoint a representative from the faculty of each of the seven undergraduate schools. In addition, the dean of the Graduate School, the college treasurer, and the college librarian would serve on the board.

James Denison's many gifts included a sense of history. In his annual reports reviewing what board members already knew about the Press's activities, he often apologized for repetitions. "Historians of the future," he invariably insisted, might have some interest in the Press. It is not surprising, then, that Denison would arrange the publication of a Press history in 1950, just three years after it was founded. The history, a brief, nine-page booklet, described the organization's bureaucratic birth; explained its governance, policies, and procedures; and even included a section on the preparation of manuscripts. Aside from future historians, the audience appears to have been Michigan State College faculty, professors elsewhere who might have a manuscript in the works, or graduate students with significant dissertations under way.

In addition to clarifying its publishing procedures, the mini-history chronicled the Press's early achievements and struggled for a definition of purpose, a statement about the special character of a college rather than a commercial press. During its brief existence, the Press's staff had published an astonishingly large number of books—approximately seventy-seven titles, in addition to laboratory manuals, course outlines, and textbooks.

By 1950, then, Michigan State College Press was firmly established. The $50,000 originally advanced from the State Board of Agriculture had been repaid. The Press was a corporation; it had a director, James Denison; it even had a published history. New offices were established in the basement of Berkey Hall and a new managing editor, William Rutter, was hired.

Denison's short history of the Press reflected, however, some uncertainty. Amid the self-congratulatory chronicle of achievements, one senses some unresolved issues, some potential for conflict, contradiction, even corruption. The titles proudly described in the history suggest something of the varied problems and pressures that would shape the Press's destiny.

The first books published seemed to deliver what the foreword to the history promised: "manuscripts from the whole field of scholarship," which would reflect "the true character of the college." In November 1947, for example, the Press published its first non-textbook title, *A Correlation of Some Physical Properties of Alkane and Alkenes*, by Ralph C. Huston, dean of the Graduate School and exofficio member of the Press's Board of Directors. The dean's book, for which publication costs had been prepaid, was accepted as a "substantial gift" to the Press. It never made it to the best-seller lists, but it did generate some badly needed revenue.

In December 1948 the Press decided "to encourage" Mentor Williams of the University of Chicago to prepare two volumes of the journals of Henry Rowe Schoolcraft, explorer and recorder of Indian lore. These Schoolcraft volumes would become the first of a series of titles dealing with "regional" topics that were of national interest. The following year, the Press also published *Fettered Freedom: Civil Liberties and the Slavery Controversy*, by Russel Nye.

The Nye book suggests a lot about the high standards and independence of the young Press. Four years earlier, in 1945, Nye had won the Pulitzer Prize for his biography *George Bancroft: Brahmin Rebel*.

Russel Nye (left) presents a copy of *Fettered Freedom* to James H. Denison

Because Nye had received a Knopf Fellowship of $1,200 to assist in his research for this work, he had a contractual obligation to offer his next two books to the Alfred Knopf publishing house. After *Fettered Freedom* was completed, however, both the author and his Knopf editors concluded that the manuscript was a specialized study more suitable for publication by a university press.

One might expect that a newly established press would have eagerly accepted the work of college faculty member whose previous book had won a prestigious national award. Instead, Nye's manuscript was subjected to intense scrutiny. It was carefully read by members of the Press's editorial board and then evaluated by two outside readers, Professor Clement Eaton of the University of Kentucky and Arthur Schlesinger Jr. of Harvard University. Schlesinger pronounced the study to be "a valuable scholarly contribution both to the history of the anti-slavery movement and to the history of our tradition of civil liberties."

The publication of *Fettered Freedom* brought the small scholarly publishing operation the prestige of a Pulitzer Prize-winning author, along with Nye's continued support and loyalty. Over the years the Press would publish three other Nye books, *Midwestern Progressive Politics* (1948), *A Baker's Dozen* (1957), and *This Almost Chosen People: Essays in American Ideas* (1966). Nye also would serve as a member of the Press's Board of Directors. In addition, he became an unofficial acquisitions editor, public relations consultant, manuscript reader, and editor. After 1949—when he secured a Rockefeller Foundation grant for Midwestern studies—he was able to contribute financially to the publication of David Meade's *Yankee Eloquence in the Middle West* (1951), Guy Cardwell's *Twins of Genius* (1953), Charles Hirschfeld's *The Great Railroad Conspiracy: The Social History of a Railroad War* (1953), and Bernard Duffy's *Chicago Renaissance* (1954). Nye wrote introductions to L. Frank Baum's *The Wizard of Oz and Who He Was* (1957), the Michigan State University Press edition of Richard Henry Dana's *Two Years Before the Mast*, and *The Diary of James Strang* (1961). Russel Nye's final service to the Press was to do the job that James Denison, who died in 1975, would have done: rewrite and edit the dictated tape-recorded memoirs of John Hannah.

The rigorous evaluation of Nye's manuscript with the help of distinguished outside readers suggests that Michigan State College Press had aspirations of truly national significance. The existence of other publications in its list suggest somewhat smaller, less purely intellectual, and frankly financial and political concerns. Thus, the anonymous authors of the Press's first history, even as they proudly described the amazing progress of their publishing house, seemed to sense some of the contradictions inherent in any academic publishing; their brief history is, in part, an attempt to clarify the unique purpose of subsidized, scholarly publishing.

Because of its guaranteed income from college subsidies, in fact the revenue from textbook sales to captive student consumers, Michigan

State College Press anticipated freedom from commercial constraints. The new Press, indeed any college press, did not need the big block-buster, the best-seller that would appeal to millions. Its aim, instead, would be to maintain a backlist of titles that would enjoy modest but steady long-term sales. All books, it was hoped, might meet their own expenses, pay their own costs, but with scholarly works success would have to be measured by long-term influence rather than short-term financial gain. Freedom from commercial concerns meant that, from the start "social service not profit must be the aim of the college press."

The founders knew that scholars and writers are not necessarily the same people. They realized, however, that no harm would be done "if they become more like one another." The Press's editors insisted, then, that scholars' prose be more lucid, possibly even appealing to nonspecialized readers. By publishing the results of scholarship they wanted to serve the faculty without becoming its servant, a vanity press, or a "glorified mimeographing office."

The Board of Directors of the new publishing corporation recognized their responsibilities to the college, the faculty, the state, and the region. An academic press, they asserted, should reflect "the true character" of the college; it should also enhance the prestige of the school, and maybe even help in recruitment by attracting "vital minds" to the campus.

Michigan State College Press should be, the directors felt, in part, a regional publisher, but this service to the region did not preclude service to the nation. As Fred Reeve, chair of the editorial committee, put it in a 1948 letter to Mentor Williams, the Press could be "primarily regional, though not primarily provincial." Even as a corporation, the Press insisted on the same academic freedom enjoyed by traditional academic departments; they claimed, that is, the freedom to publish "works that contain facts that may be unpleasant or distasteful to segments of the population, special interests and so forth." This abstract defense of free speech did not, as it turned out, mean that the Press would always respect the academic freedom of students nor that it would welcome internal criticism that might reveal "unpleasant and distasteful facts" about academic publishing.

A DANGEROUS OPINION

By 1950 Michigan State College Press had reached the point where it could employ a full-time managing editor to assist its badly overworked director, James Denison. William Rutter, a young rising star from the

William Rutter

scholarly publishing world, was chosen to fill this new position. Although he served for only sixteen months, he left behind a remarkable record of his editing skill and put in place a set of exemplary professional principles. Rutter, for example, brought Michigan State College Press into the Association of American University Presses (AAUP), the national association for a unique and often puzzling profession. The AAUP had been founded in 1938 to establish standards for university presses and to share information about the special problems inherent in nonprofit, subsidized scholarly publishing. In a letter to Morton Bloomfield, the author of *The*

Seven Deadly Sins, Rutter mentioned his attendance at an AAUP meeting in Toronto. "Encouraged" by the session on scholarly writing, Rutter proceeded to pass on some advice about audience and style. Bloomfield, in his first chapter, was trying to respond to two different audiences—the nonspecialist, who needed a review of scholarship, and his scholarly peers, who would resent any attempt to oversimplify a complex body of knowledge. Rutter advised him to "make assumptions of knowledge," and "allow the nonspecialist who reads your book to find the basis of such assumptions through further study."

Rutter had previously served as an assistant to the president of Oxford University Press. He had, as a result of this experience, a definite notion of what, ideally, academic publishing should be. On 5 October 1950, he defined this sense of a university press in a letter to Reul Denny, the University of Chicago sociologist and poet.

Denny, along with David Reisman and Nathan Glazer, had just published *The Lonely Crowd,* an enormously influential book destined to dominate American thought throughout the next decade. To Denny, Rutter expressed his interest in significant books that dealt with "some of the undercurrents that shift society." The ideal university press book, he asserted, would be a book like *The Lonely Crowd,* a book that could serve "as a bridge between the university and the intelligent layman."

Another ideal university press title, one brought to Michigan State College Press by Russel Nye, was Herbert Weisinger's *Tragedy and Paradox of the Fortunate Fall.* Weisinger had started the manuscript while a member of the Princeton Institute for Advanced Studies and had completed it while a senior research fellow at the Warburg Institute; the work was enthusiastically recommended by Herbert Read, the British poet-critic. Weisinger, in a letter to William Rutter, expressed the hope that, when published, his book might "add something to the prestige of the MSC Press."

Weisinger's manuscript was considered for publication, along with another entitled *The Cross Sectional Nomenclature of the Beef Carcass.* While the beef carcass book was unanimously approved by the Press's board, Weisinger's classic study received a dissenting vote. The minutes of this Board of Directors meeting suggest the unavoidable tensions of running a scholarly press at a land-grant college, a place where the study of agriculture and the humanities coexisted uneasily.

When these internal tensions came into conflict with the overheated zeal of mid-century American national politics, William Rutter's publishing principles would clash with James Denison's public relations concerns.

The conflict, ignited by an editorial in the Michigan State College student newspaper, would ultimately clarify the Press's publishing role and would, most importantly, contribute to the education of President John Hannah. As a young man he had dropped out of the University of Michigan's law school in 1920; now, thirty years later, he would be subjected to a crash course in constitutional law.

John Hannah, of course, was not the only liberal college president to experience firsthand what came to be called "the Great Fear." The spring of 1950 was an exceedingly uncomfortable and uncertain time for all Americans. Senator Joseph McCarthy's reckless anti-Communism had spread across the nation, infecting college presidents, as well as semiprofessional patriots. The University of California imposed loyalty oaths on its employees and dismissed 157 who refused to sign. The National Association for the Advancement of Colored People, at its convention in Boston, formally resolved to purge its leadership of communists. On 27 June President Truman decided to resist North Korea's invasion of the South and halt the advance of an apparent Communist juggernaut in the Far East. From a national perspective, the events that would shake the college in East Lansing can be seen as a local expression of these larger, more powerful forces operating at the national and international levels.

For the previous thirteen years the Michigan American Legion had held its annual Boy's State Convention on the Michigan State College campus. At its 1950 gathering, the Legion staged a mock trial of a hypothetical American citizen accused of perjury for denying that he was a Communist. This fantasy legal proceeding conducted in the imaginary Boy's State had some dramatic real world consequences after it inspired an unsigned editorial in Michigan State College's student newspaper, the *State News*. The anonymously published piece in question, titled "It's Not the Way," appeared on 22 June, just before the end of spring semester. After describing the intense anti-Communist Boy's State atmosphere and the boisterous kangaroo court that had been conducted there, the editorial writer concluded with a criticism of the American Legion's "narrow principles, bald faced fascism, and militaristic ideas."

The Legion's leadership, of course, protested. Meeting in Sault Ste. Marie, on Michigan's Upper Peninsula, the organization passed a resolution calling for a legislative investigation. The editorial, in the Legion's view, seemed to show "the hand of an expert in the sinister technique of subverting our American institutions."

The Michigan State College administration's response was swift, hysterical, and totalitarian. President Hannah issued a formal apology to the

American Legion and shut down the *State News* for the summer. When student editors Ron Litton and Hal Willard considered publishing an independent newspaper, they were warned by faculty advisor A. A. Applegate that they would be expelled from school if they did. After consulting with an admired Lansing lawyer, John Brattin, the young journalists appealed to news professionals across the state. This effort to "drum up a pressure group of our own to combat the American Legion" increased the tensions within Hannah's office. One result was "A Petition Respectfully Submitted to President Hannah." The petitioners, all Michigan State College staff members, urged that the paper "be immediately allowed to resume publication." The petitioners argued:

First, MSC needs a publication which reports news and airs opinion.

Second, Regardless of the quality of the editorial written, we feel that suspension of the paper is not justified. The democratic way recognizes complete freedom of speech, thought, and press. When a student newspaper differs from the administration, faculty, or outside opinion, the solution is not to suspend the newspaper. Instead, space should be given to whoever differs with its published opinions.

Third, We as university staff members cannot continue to speak in the classroom about freedom of the press and see it denied to our students.

Fourth, MSC has gained stature in recent years and can well afford to resist outside pressures. We feel the college has already suffered adverse publicity and will suffer more unless this ban is rescinded.

The document was signed by 238 people, including Russell Kirk, Russel Nye, and William Rutter. All of the signers identified themselves by title and department. An anonymous administration functionary noted additional information about the petitioners; "31 of MSC['s] staff attended Teachers Union Conference."

Hannah was rigid and unyielding with the faculty members who had implored him to reverse his decision. Russel Nye, for example, left an angry meeting with the president convinced that he no longer had a future at Michigan State. With students, however, Hannah was conciliatory, sympathetic, or at least convincingly manipulative. He invited editor Ron Litton to his presidential residence, Cowles House, for a private conversation. To young Litton, the college president seemed "to let his hair down." He gave the impression that "he hates himself because he could not fight these guys." If the editorial had only been "more temperate," he would have "fought for the students." Litton was convinced that "Hannah and the school and the Legion were hurt more than we ever were." Hannah, he believed, had given instructions "to administration figureheads not to touch this paper."

The following October, the author of the controversial editorial, the "expert in the sinister technique of subverting American institutions," returned to the Michigan State College campus to begin graduate study in English. Russell McKee was a twenty-five-year-old U. S. Army veteran who had served in Europe during World War II. After writing the offending editorial the previous June, McKee had gone off to work for a Middleton, New York, newspaper for the summer. His friends Litton and Willard had kept him informed of the controversy through letters, telegrams, and news clippings, but he had no real sense of the vindictive rage his editorial had aroused until he returned to East Lansing in the fall. To defray the expenses of graduate study, young McKee had taken two jobs, a night editor's position at the *State News* and a part-time publicist's job at Michigan State College Press.

At the first MSC Board of Publications meeting in the fall of 1950, James Denison and Philip May, the college's controller, assailed McKee. "What about McKee?" they wanted to know. Was it safe to have him on the student paper? The Publications Board, as Tom Nicolson reported in his *State News* "Men and Principles" column on 17 October, decided that McKee would work only until another staff member could be trained to take his place.

To Denison, McKee's editorial was "a flagrant violation of journalistic ethics, good manners and sound newspaper practices." When he learned that the author of the "explosive" editorial was employed at Michigan State College Press as well, he instructed his managing editor to fire him. Rutter carried out the order and dismissed McKee, but objected strenuously to the suggestion that "the student was not hired in the first place because he was not hired by an authorized person." This phrase, designed no doubt to cover up a clear violation of McKee's First Amendment rights, raised disturbing questions about the managing editor's authority.

Rutter responded to these events on 25 October 1950 with an extraordinary three-page memo to the Michigan State College Press Board of Directors. Titled "Duties of the Managing Editor," the memo began with a candid summary of the McKee affair. Russell McKee, Rutter explained, "is the only student who has evinced any interest in book work and the work of the Press, and I make no apology for hiring him. I knew that he

Russell McKee

had written the so-called explosive editorial this summer, but I assumed that he was not to be punished for this editorial beyond what had already happened."

After describing his role in the hiring—and firing—of young McKee, Rutter continued with an eloquent personal testimony ("I believe in books") and a demand for clarification of his authority. He had assumed, Rutter continued, that he was a responsible executive of the Press. He had, therefore, made commitments to individuals, specifically Frederick Hoffman, who was preparing a collection of Faulkner criticism, and Sherwood Anderson's widow, who was negotiating for the publication of her husband's letters. Rutter, insisting on clearly defined duties for the managing editor, reminded the board that "the caliber of the press represents the caliber of the university."

Unwilling to accept responsibility without authority, Rutter soon resigned as managing editor and went off to India as an editor for the State Department.[7] Before he left for his new post, however, he presented his "General Statement on the Status of the Press" to the Board of Directors. His final report is an extraordinary, prescient document; it offers impressive evidence that departing executives' farewell statements, like deathbed confessions, have a special credibility. Institutions would be well advised to pay attention to those on the way out, especially to those like Dumas Malone and William Rutter, who leave without personal agendas or ambitions.

Acknowledging that he had served for only sixteen months, Rutter explained that he had done a lot of listening in an attempt to measure the reaction of faculty and administration toward the Press. In his listening, Rutter explained, he heard, again and again, one "dangerous opinion":

> the Michigan College Press is supported by the Basic College textbooks and that our profits from the selling of these textbooks to an assured market guarantees us a large subsidy for the publication of scholarly works.

There was, of course, some truth in this "dangerous opinion." A Basic College text for a required course such as Effective Living yielded a return of $5,950, while Written and Spoken English, another required course, brought in $4,949.65. These were substantial sums in the early 1950s and, when combined with other texts, manuals, and syllabi, amounted to an $18,000 annual income or "subsidy" from the Basic College's standardized monopoly of undergraduate education.

The danger in this opinion, Rutter explained, was that "the Basic College faculty feel that their toil and the students' money were supporting an institution imposed on them." The result was continual requests for complimentary copies and endless demands for revisions from a press whose most visible and profitable mission appeared to be faculty support services.

William Rutter was clearly skeptical about the "subsidy"; he even questioned "if it is desirable to call it that." He wanted to deemphasize the textbook business and stress the value of a backlist, a slow but steady source of long-term income. Russel Nye's *Fettered Freedom* had at this point earned a negligible amount, but it had, Rutter insisted, the possibility of modest, long-term sales. An academic press, Rutter concluded, "must look to the point where at least half, and preferably over half, of its income each year must come from the backlist."

Rutter is blunt and eloquent on the subject of financing. "We must," he insisted, "face one axiom at the Michigan State College Press; we shall have financial difficulties for many years, and we must realize, and permit the university to realize, that a university press has a long range nature." Rutter confronted the question, "Where do we get the money to pay the bills?" His answer, again, was the backlist. "The great English universities," he instructed the Board, "had a great book on their backlists: The Bible." Michigan State College Press had no such best-seller, but, he said, the Nye book and others "will sell long past the time we are able to write off their costs."

The problem of publishing, Rutter explained, was in part an accounting problem; production costs showed up as losses long before accounts receivable could indicate any profit.

> For such financial stability we need, perhaps even more than money, patience. It may take five years, it may take ten years, and it may take fifteen years before we reach such a point, but this does not mean we cannot be active within this period. We must be cautious to the point that every book we take on must either have the quality of long life and excellence, or it must have the character that meets our editorial requirements and will sell out within a few years at a profit if it cannot stand the long run.

The Rutter report is, in retrospect, an extraordinary analysis, an X-ray revealing serious economic and institutional flaws. These problems, however abstract in 1950, would eventually multiply and metastasize until decades later they would threaten the very existence of the Press.

Even after his resignation Rutter fought for a professional scholarly press at Michigan State. The minutes of the Board of Directors' meeting of 24 January 1951 record an almost Browningesque dialogue between Rutter and Denison that raised some fundamental—and enduring—issues. At this meeting the managing editor and the director articulated the different perspectives that had contributed to William Rutter's resignation.

Early in the meeting Denison expressed his concern that the Press was "trying to go ahead too fast for the capital we have." When the possibility of another $50,000 loan was raised, Rutter responded that the Press must be maintained "with a constant subsidy." When someone observed that 1950 was a bad year, Rutter predicted that "we will have ten bad years." Financial loss was the nature of academic publishing, Rutter explained. "If there wasn't a risk in publishing the type of books university presses do, there would be no university presses. Commercial publishers would do it."

Denison continued to worry about money. He feared that the State Board of Agriculture had been deceived. Michigan State College Press, he insisted, was not supposed to be a press in this new sense.

When asked what other presses did about their deficits, Rutter explained that "some large presses do trade books. Some have endowments. Some have outright subsidies." These were certainly "unpleasant and distasteful facts," and they no doubt contributed to the strained relationship between the director and the managing editor.

There is no evidence that William Rutter, his terse comments during this meeting, or his two eloquent reports were taken seriously. The following year, after Rutter had escaped to India, the same confusion about authority, and the same uncertainty about academic publishing came up again when the Press rejected a manuscript by Richard Dorson.

Richard Dorson, an associate professor at Michigan State College, was making an international reputation as a folklorist. He had already published three books, and the rejection of his manuscript, a study of folk tales from Michigan's Upper Peninsula, was understandably distressing. The rejection inspired an angry but insightful five-page critique of the Press.

Dorson was obviously annoyed that his manuscript, "originally solicited with a virtual promise of publication," was rejected after a nine-month delay on the grounds of "faulty scholarship." This criticism, Dorson reminded the board, overlooked his scholarly apparatus, the footnotes contained in an appendix that was lost by the Press. Also overlooked was Dorson's five-year campaign against what he called the popularized "fakelore" of other scholars in the field.

Dorson's experience with the Michigan State College Press was certainly disappointing. His report reiterated some familiar facts that were "unpleasant and distasteful." The Dorson report singled out two "most unfortunate features"—"the heterogeneous nature of the Board and the division of responsibility in the press."

The Board of Directors' meeting of 22 February 1951, which considered Dorson's criticism, offers documentary evidence of the accuracy of his complaints. One board member, A. A. Applegate, raised the question, mercilessly cemented into the minutes, "What is folklore? Is it stories taken from comic books and put into the mouths of characters?"

The Dorson letter, like the Rutter report, was an insightful, thoughtful, potentially educational critique. It was, the board minutes noted, "received, considered and filed." Three months later Richard Dorson had the pleasure of informing the Michigan State College Press Editorial

Board that Harvard University Press would be publishing his book, "without request for documentation." Shortly after Harvard published his *Bloodstoppers and Bearwalkers: Folk Traditions of the Upper Peninsula*, Dorson resigned from Michigan State College and accepted a professorship at Indiana University.

JAMES DENISON'S LEGACY

For all its growing pains, financial restraints, and indifference to constructive criticism, Michigan State College Press under James Denison's leadership published some outstanding scholarship. Charles Hirschfield's *The Great Railroad Conspiracy* (1953) chronicled the struggle of Michigan farmers to gain compensation for the killing of their livestock by trains. Although this book was strictly regional history, it delighted reviewers, including Eric Goldman, the future White House intellectual-in-residence who would write *The Tragedy of Lyndon Johnson* in 1969. Goldman recommended the Hirschfield study to readers of *The Key Reporter* as "a little gem of historical craftsmanship."

David Mead's *Yankee Eloquence in the Middle West: The Ohio Lyceum, 1850–1870* was another regional but by no means provincial study of a specialized scholarly subject. Originally a dissertation written at Ohio State University, Mead's book earned reviews from three giants of American Studies, Robert Spiller, Carl Bode, and Harry Hayden Clark. Spiller's review, although not uncritical, recommended the book to readers of *The American Society of Political and Social Science Annals* as "a thorough job." Bode, reviewing for *The American Quarterly*, hailed *Yankee Eloquence* "as the first really thorough and detailed study of the lyceum system in any part of the country." Harry Hayden Clark, writing in *The American Historical Review*, praised Mead's study as "judicious, meaty, comprehensive, and a model for similar studies which might be made of the lyceum system in other western states."

Russell Nye's *Midwestern Progressive Politics* (1951) was in many ways the ideal college press book. Written by a Michigan State faculty member, it dealt with a regional topic of national significance. Harry Stevens, writing in *The South Atlantic Quarterly*, hailed it as "an outstanding achievement of neo-Turnian historical writing." Professor William Hesseltine, a former teacher of Nye's at the University of Wisconsin, recommended the work in *The Progressive* as "a brilliant summary of a significant political movement." *The New York Times* reviewer, Richard Hofstader, identified Nye's unique "flair for broad synthesis and for readable narrative." Nye, he concluded,

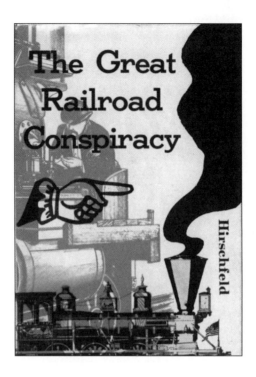

Charles Hirschfield's *The Great Railroad Conspiracy* **(1953)**

"executes with unusual success an exceptionally difficult and important assignment."

Other notable books from the Denison years include Frank Woodford's *Mister Jefferson's Disciple* (1953), a biography of the first Chief Justice of the Michigan Territory, and Lester Crocker's *The Embattled Philosopher* (1954). The first biography of Diderot to appear in English during the twentieth century, *The Embattled Philosopher* earned a review from Cyril Connolly in *The Times* of London.

In addition to these outstanding titles, the young Press began to develop a speciality in medieval studies. The 1952 publication of William Heist's *The Fifteen Signs before Doomsday* and Arnold Williams's *The Characterization of Pilate in the Townely Plays* enhanced the Press's reputation in this area. Williams's book was well received in scholarly circles and praised in *Modern Language Review* as "one of the most fascinating and important contributions to the subject." Williams's book was, moreover, an attractively designed, aesthetically pleasing object. It was the first Press book designed

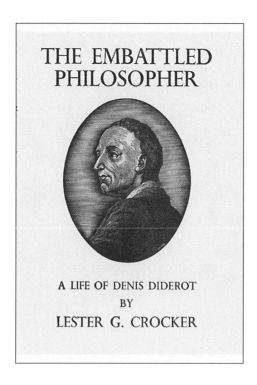

THE EMBATTLED
PHILOSOPHER

A LIFE OF DENIS DIDEROT
BY
LESTER G. CROCKER

Lester Crocker's *The Embattled Philosopher* **(1954)**

by Charles Pollack, the brother of Jackson Pollack, who taught in the art department and served the Press as "typographic consultant."

The Arnold Williams book also helped to attract Morton Bloomfield's classic study, *The Seven Deadly Sins*. Bloomfield, an associate professor at Ohio State, had originally found a publisher at the Harvard University Press. When James Denison expressed amazement that Bloomfield would prefer Michigan State College's small, relatively obscure press to Harvard's, William Rutter responded with a memo. Michigan State's request of a $1,840 contribution from the author was $500 less than Harvard's demand for a "subvention." Beyond the financial advantage, Rutter pointed out, "obviously, on a manuscript of limited appeal such as this, we can do just as good a job as Harvard on circulating the book. There is also the possibility that, because of the friendship with Professor Williams and Professor Heist, he looks with favor upon our efforts in the medieval period."

Rutter's brief memo says a lot about the relationship between a scholarly press and a scholarly faculty. A strong faculty makes for a strong press and a strong press, in turn, strengthens the faculty. In other words, an academic press both reflects and reinforces the strength of academic departments. The Press attracts distinguished books and these books then help to attract and retain distinguished faculty. The press and the departments are, on this level, operating in an intimate, mutually rewarding partnership. Their relationship is far more complex, more symbiotic, than an undergraduate department's need for printing services.

Chapter 2

"AN INTERESTING FELLOW"

In 1952, after William Rutter's eloquent exit, James Denison found another managing editor, a remarkable young Australian. Lyle Blair at thirty-five was the kind of man who inspired myths. The details of his life were certainly dramatic, maybe even a bit melodramatic. Blair, it was rumored, had left his native Australia in 1935 under extraordinary circumstances—he had run off to England with an opera singer.

In London he served his apprenticeship in publishing under Jonathan Cape, the distinguished publisher of D. H. Lawrence, Robert Graves, and Malcolm Lowry.[1] (Years later Blair would name his son Jonathan after the old publisher he called "my master.") During World War II he had been an RAF pilot and at some point he had engaged in top-secret, high-level espionage in the Middle East. After the war he served as diplomatic correspondent for the *London Graphic*, general manager of the British Publishers Guild, and director of Pocket Books, G.R.

THE BLAIR LEGEND

Aside from the episode with the opera singer, who left no paper trail, Lyle Blair's reputation as a swashbuckling adventurer appears to be remarkably consistent with his documented life. Press archives show that Blair enjoyed easy access to the highest levels of the Anglo-Australian political establishment during his years at Michigan State University. For example, in 1953, when President Hannah, then serving as assistant secretary of defense, was traveling the globe, Blair sought to smooth his way. In a 6 October memo to Denison, Blair hinted at his romantic past.

> I have alerted diplomatic missions in Tokyo, Hong Kong, Saigon and London regarding President Hannah's forthcoming visit. Also, a letter will be awaiting at the Savoy from Miss de Zouche offering her services.
>
> The American Ambassador in Cairo is an old friend of mine. It is not beyond the bounds of possibilities that he will be in Beirut when President

Hannah pays his visit. If so, the Ambassador might be amused to know that Lyle Blair of the Middle East Intelligence Center is now a peaceful citizen on a University campus.

Two years after this memo offering the services of Mary de Zouche (a former employee of Blair's who was engaged in British publishing) Blair tried to convince Guy Howarth and A. J. M. Smith, the distinguished Canadian poet and MSU faculty member, to edit an anthology of poetry. "Our Common Tongue," as it was originally titled, would be a collection of poetry by English-speaking peoples from around the world.

As usual, Blair was eager to use old friends from his glamorous past to promote the books he planned to publish. On 11 June 1958, he wrote Sir Winston Churchill requesting a fifteen-hundred to two-thousand-word introduction to the anthology. He offered a $750.00 advance with a 2 percent royalty on all copies sold. Sir Winston, responding through a secretary, declined this generous offer, but it was noted that "your thought of him nevertheless gave Sir Winston pleasure."

The anthology was never published, but the episode serves to show Blair at his aggressive best, using the contacts of the past to promote the publishing interests of the present. Blair was never timid about approaching the great. In 1959 he succeeded in getting Eleanor Roosevelt to write a charming preface for a children's book, *La Citadelle Enchantée,* by Isabelle Georges Schreiber.

Although the overture to Churchill might seem fanciful, even risible, it was serious. In another 1958 letter to the Honorable R. G. Casey, the Australian minister for internal affairs, Blair wrote:

> The enclosed carbon of my letter to Sir Winston Churchill is self-explanatory. I do hope that he will see fit to undertake this, although I cannot remember him ever expressing any particular liking for poetry. Nevertheless, this is an important book, not only in America, but throughout the world.
>
> Talking of Sir Winston reminds me that I was looking through some old negatives the other day and had the enclosed printed up. This was taken at the Damascus Intelligence Centre when you were Minister of State in the Middle East. I have no doubt you will remember on the left Air Commodore Buss, who was for some time your advisor of Arab affairs, and next to him Colonel Willie Elphinstone, the Queen Mother's cousin. Next to me is Brian Guiness, the son of your former deputy, the last Lord Moyne. Things have changed since then.

Lyle Blair

The legend of Lyle Blair was also enlarged by his "absolute block against supplying biographical data," and his self-amused, self-deprecatory sense of humor, which was invariably stimulated by ceremonies and honors. In 1962, for example, the University of Michigan sought to honor him for organizing the first publishing house in Austria to print "books which had fallen under the Nazi ban." Blair, responding to the university's request for cap and gown measurements, offered this modest self-portrait: "I am a rather miserable little man standing five foot seven, with far too small a chest and probably far too large a head."

In similar style, Blair recalled his initial hiring at the Press in a taped, 1985 dinner of the Press Committee. He had come to East Lansing to give a lecture at an English Department event. After his talk he had gotten drunk at a faculty party. When he sobered up the next day, he learned that he had been offered—and had accepted—a job as managing editor of the Press.

However inauspicious his beginning at the Press, Blair eventually won the respect and confidence of John Hannah and James Denison. In 1969, Hannah, with uncharacteristic understatement, would introduce Lyle Blair to his successor, President-select Clifton Wharton Jr., as "an interesting fellow." In the same 12 November 1969 letter, Hannah, now director of the Agency for International Development in the Nixon administration, credited Blair with building "the MSU Press from nothing to one of the outstanding university presses in America. What is more extraordinary is that he made it pay its own way every step of the road. He is exceedingly competent. You will never have known anyone quite like him but you can count on him to get his job done well."

The competence and uniqueness that so impressed President Hannah are evident in the monthly reports the new managing editor was required, at first, to make. These chatty and charming documents are like vivid snapshots of the audacious young editor in action. Blair, for example, meets Illinois Senator Paul Douglas at a booksellers' convention in Chicago. The senator makes "warm references" to Russel Nye's *Midwestern Progressive Politics*. Blair, as soon as he returns to East Lansing, sends the senator complimentary copies of Nye's book, along with a request to quote the "warm references" in ads. He approaches Frank Lloyd Wright and urges him to write a book "on the place of the artist in modern society." James Denison is cool to this project, so Blair abandons the idea and goes off in pursuit of Irma Rombauer, the author of that lucrative classic *The Joy of Cooking*. Blair's scheme for a Midwestern cookbook fails to inspire Mrs. Rombauer.

ACQUIRING A REPUTATION

From the first day on the job Blair was independent and determined to maintain the highest standards. A book submitted through President Hannah was bluntly dismissed, "as one of the worst manuscripts I have seen in my life." Another book (submitted by a man named Grace) prompted Blair to share his scorn with Denison and the board: "One needs a certain amount of grace not to explode at a book of this type

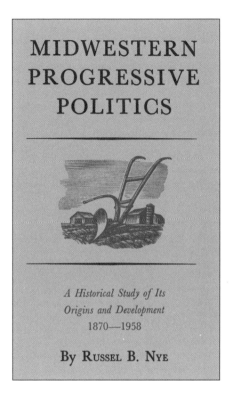

Russell Nye's *Midwestern Progressive Politics*

being submitted to a university press. It is written by a psychologist trying to be Norman Vincent Peale and is aimed at the mass public for whom self-delusion is a religion."

Of course, not all of Blair's decisions were wise. His anti-Communism once caused him to reject Nelson Algren's *A Walk on the Wild Side.* Blair's comments about this novel suggest that he had by 1954 learned something about public relations from James Denison. Algren's novel, he wrote, was "great fun," and "a fairly successful endeavor to tear to pieces the *Saturday Evening Post* mentality. Unfortunately, the author drifts into the realm of politics, and although no Marxist, he might well be considered a subversive by some of the more conservative members of the State Legislature." As a representative of a state-supported university, he concluded, "this book is not our cup of tea."

From the details in the monthly reports, we can estimate Blair's initial influence on the Press. In the three years he was managing editor the

Press began to attract British and Australian authors. In addition, the books that were under way when Blair arrived began to be reviewed in very impressive publications, national and international, by some very impressive persons. Lester Crocker's biography of Diderot, for example, got reviewed by Albert Guerard in *Saturday Review* and Cyril Connally in the *London Sunday Times*.

It can be said, moreover, that Blair, from the beginning, literally made his mark on the Press. Henceforth the books he published would be adorned with *his* distinctive logo—the sign of the Southern Cross, which appears on the Australian flag. The books with this five-star symbolic signature reflected Blair's enormous pride in publishing and his growing influence at the Press.

The value of Blair's transcontinental connections was acknowledged in James Denison's 1954 report to the Board of Directors. The managing editor, Denison announced, was largely responsible for the best year in the Press's history. Lyle Blair, he continued, "has brought to the Press a degree of professional competence never before available to us, and we have profited greatly from his acquaintance with publishers and authors in the commercial and academic fields alike."

Nineteen hundred and fifty-four had been a good year for the Press; Denison could boast that the Press had published nineteen trade books and that *The New York Times* had reviewed or would review every book on the fall list. In reporting on these books, Denison did not hesitate to compare his small college press to the University of Chicago Press, a giant in university publishing. "We are," Denison exalted, "now publishing more trade books than the University of Chicago Press, and the turnover of our new books is greater than the turnover on their new books."

One of the earliest and most exotic fruits of Blair's British connections involved some *fin de siècle* figures, Rex Warner, Frank Harris, Oscar Wilde, and A. J. A. Symonds. Rex Warner was an old friend of Blair's and in 1951 they had written a book about British football together, *Ashes to Ashes*, a book with an intriguing title but (to Americans) an incomprehensible content. Warner, like Blair, had escaped the bleakness of postwar England, and was now ensconced at the University of Connecticut. Warner's books *Greeks and Trojans* (1953) and *The Vengeance of the Gods* (1955) were among the first to sport the southern cross.

Unlike the Warner books, which attracted little attention, Frank Harris's biography of Oscar Wilde linked the Michigan State press with one of the most scandalous figures of the late Victorian period. In 1916 Frank Harris, an American literary adventurer, had published *Oscar Wilde:*

His Life and Confessions in the United States. Although H. L. Mencken had praised the book as "perhaps the best biography ever done by an American," the book had been banned in England because it incorporated all of Wilde's allegations concerning his homosexual lover, Lord Alfred Douglas.

Michigan State University's 1959 edition of Harris's unexpurgated text included an essay by George Bernard Shaw, "Memories of Wilde," and an introductory note by the editor. The editor, apparently anticipating controversy on the conservative campus, identified himself as "Mr. Lyle Blair of New South Wales," but the biography raised no eyebrows and caused no public relations problems. In fact, the MSU Press's belated publicizing of the sordid Wilde scandal resulted in some very gratifying national recognition. The book carned enthusiastic reviews in the *Saturday Review* and it was selected by the Mid-Century Bookclub as the July Book-of-the-Month. This splendid little book club, founded by Sol Stein, offered its members a most selective and discriminating choice of books. Its monthly brochure was itself an elegant and unique publication featuring short review-essays by members of the editorial board—W. H. Auden, Jaques Barzun, and Lionel Trilling.

Lyle Blair's pride in seeing an MSU book selected by this distinguished book club, and reviewed in its brochure by Barzun, was communicated to the Press Board of Directors in his annual report. His more moving and spontaneous statement was written on the back of Mid-Century's brochure:

> This may be too much to expect from an ed. system which has so radically neglected the teaching of our own language.

The *succès d'estime* enjoyed by Frank Harris's biography of Oscar Wilde inspired yet another venture into late Victorian erotica, a proposed new edition of Harris's racy autobiography, *My Life and Loves*. Both Blair and his new assistant, Jack Gallagher, were enthusiastic about the book. Blair's introduction to the Harris biography of Wilde had announced the "anticipated" publication of Harris's autobiography. Gallagher, in a letter to Jacques Barzun, could scarcely contain his enthusiasm. After offering Barzun "Greetings from practically nowhere," Gallagher shared his excitement about the forthcoming book. "We have," he wrote, "the volumes which Harris himself marked in his own hand the passages for expurgation."

For all the enthusiasm, Frank Harris's edition was never published by the MSU Press. Four years later, after he left MSU to accept a position at St. Martin's Press, Gallagher would edit and write the introduction to

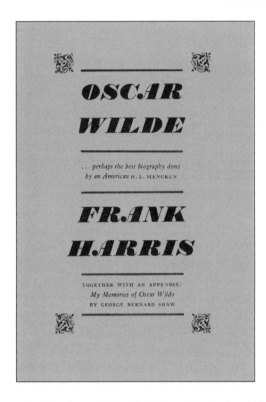

Frank Harris's *Oscar Wilde: His Life and Confessions* **(1959)**

Grove Press's edition of *My Life and Loves,* now subtitled "Five volumes in one/complete and unexpurgated."

Frank Harris's sexual autobiography may have been incompatible with Blair's highly developed sense of decorum. The director of MSU Libraries, Richard Chapin, who sought the Harris materials for Special Collections, recalled years later that Blair "kept taking the loves out of the life and Gallagher kept putting them back in." Finally, they abandoned the edition and went on to another underground classic, A. J. A. Symond's *The Quest for Corvo.*[2]

Written in 1934 and published for the first time in America by the MSU Press, *The Quest for Corvo* was a curiously modern biography that emphasized the author's search for biographical fact as much as the actual subject of the biography. This odd book, "a classic in the literature of hate," as Blair called it, was remarkably successful. It was reviewed enthusiastically by Gilbert Highet and eventually adopted by the Book-of-the-Month Club. In 1979 the paperback rights were sold to Penguin Books.

Frank Harris's biography of Oscar Wilde and A. J. A. Symond's *Quest for Corvo* were remarkable books for a press whose reputation was based on scholarly studies of medieval literature and technical studies of agricultural subjects. Lyle Blair "standing 5'7"," had cast a long shadow across the Atlantic. Under his leadership the Press had ventured into erotic and other potentially controversial areas that would not be fully exploited until Ralph Ginzburg founded the notorious and litigious Grove Press. Moreover, the Press had become a determined, curiously elitist institution coexisting peacefully—and maybe unnoticed—within a populist, land-grant institution.

R. K. NARAYAN

Of all the authors Blair brought to the Michigan State University Press, the most distinguished was the Indian novelist R. K. Narayan. Certainly no other MSU Press author had ever been profiled in the *New Yorker* or seriously discussed as a potential Nobel Prize winner. Narayan was originally discovered by Blair's friend Graham Greene, the British novelist. Greene convinced Blair, who in turn convinced James Denison, that Narayan deserved an American audience. In 1953, then, Michigan State's press published *Grateful to Life and Death*, its first novel and among the first fiction published by American university presses.[3] Published by Greene's firm, Eyre and Spottswood, in 1944, the novel was originally titled *The English Instructor*. Blair, fearing that it might be mistaken for an educational tract, boldly retitled it with a graceful line from the novel's conclusion.

Over the next six years Blair and the Michigan State University Press published five more Narayan novels: *The Financial Expert* in 1953, *Swami and Friends* and *The Bachelor of Arts* in 1954; and two novels of Malgudi, *Waiting for the Mahatma* in 1955 and *The Printer of Malgudi* in 1957.

Blair recognized Narayan as "one of the finest writers of the 20th century," and the critics agreed. Anthony West, writing in the *New Yorker*, observed that Narayan "is a writer of Gogol's stature, with the same gift for creating atmosphere in a time of change." Ann Freemantle, writing in *Commonweal*, called Narayan "an Indian Chekov." Other critics used the term "Faulkneresque," because Narayan created or recreated an imaginary Indian world as real and vivid as Yoknapatawa County in Mississippi.[4] Lyle Blair, through his visits to Narayan, came to know that world, and when Marshall Best, the vice president of Viking Press, requested biographical information in 1958, Blair could write of Narayan:

All of his books are based on characters, many of whom I have met, residing in Mysore. For instance *The Printer of Malgudi* is Sampeth in the novel, but, I have drunk coffee with Sampeth who is a printer in Mysore and who runs the City Power Press. All the events in *The Printer* took place and the central character, Srinivas, is Narayan.

Blair's motives in promoting Narayan's American career were at first entirely altruistic. In September 1956 when Narayan was prepared for his first visit to America, Blair wrote him:

> So far we have lost many, many thousands of dollars on the publication of your books, but we are prepared to go on losing this money until such a time as a widespread public appreciates the beauty of your work. It is a great honor to be your American publisher and, believe me, although your books have not sold by the tens of thousands here, you will find a large number of enthusiastic admirers on your arrival.

Narayan's 1956 visit to the United States was a most successful one. He was lionized in New York, where he met Ved Mehta; Edward Shils, the sociologist; John Gunther, the celebrated novelist; and Greta Garbo. After visiting the MSU campus and meeting with students and faculty, he toured the country finding inspiration for another book, *The Dateless Diary*, a record of his experiences in America.

Blair's relationship with Narayan was protective, almost paternalistic, affectionate, admiring, and, at times, positively playful. A 4 April 1959, letter reveals something of the flavor of their friendship—and something too of Blair's exotic interests and mysterious enterprises. Of his forthcoming visit to Narayan, he wrote that:

> After leaving you, I must make a deviation on my trip. I must visit New Delhi after visiting Bombay and before proceeding to Karachi. Amongst other things, I want to try and arrange a meeting with the Dalai Lama. I am sure that the Maharaja of Mysore could help in this, but I understand that he is in the United States. Can you think of anybody else who could arrange this? It is really most important. I would do almost anything to have half a day with him with an adequate translator. Have you any religious strings you could pull?

Moving on to discussing business matters, Blair gently scolded Narayan for telling his British publishers that they could sell his novel *The Financial*

Expert throughout the world. "You have been very naughty," Blair wrote, and he added that "whenever you do things like this in the future, please let me know or I will become VERY ANGRY." The letter's affectionate conclusion refers to Narayan's new friends in America.

> Greta Garbo and all my harem here at the Press send you their love. For my part, I send your daughter my love, your grand-daughter my love, Sampath my love and, oh well, I will break down, you my love.

Narayan's next novel, *The Guide*, was published by Viking Press in 1958. Blair explained this change in Narayan's publishers with a note in the 13 May issue of *Publishers Weekly.* "We are," he wrote, "sad, yet proud to announce that, after the publication of *The Printer of Malgudi,* Mr Narayan's future novels will be published by the Viking Press. We feel that we have played our part in introducing Mr. Narayan to the American public and we wish the Viking Press and Mr. Narayan unlimited success in the future. And in conclusion, we would like to thank the critics who made this recognition possible." Narayan's *The Guide,* dedicated to Lyle Blair, made it to Broadway when Harvey Breit and his wife, Patricia Rhinehard, wrote a drama based on the novel. The play closed after only five performances.

Back in 1947 the founders of the MSU Press, the members of the Bookstore Committee, had hoped that there might be some "prestige value" in a college press. The publication of Narayan's novels showed the university press at its best, doing what trade publishers were, at first, unwilling to do and then, after Narayan's American reputation had been achieved, gracefully yielding to a larger publisher. A photograph of Narayan, Blair, and John Hannah taken at the Algonquin Hotel celebration of *The Guide* is an enduring tribute to a small press's ability to make a contribution to world literature and thereby gain something grander than publicity or prestige.

Lyle Blair, it might be said, had two passions—books and the celebration of books. Former members of the Board of Directors remember some of the celebrations staged at "The Boom-Boom Room," a Lansing restaurant whose bar had a Polynesian theme. One of Blair's monumental achievements as a publisher was the *Australian Encyclopedia* (1958). The publication of this huge, ten-volume project called for a monumental celebration held at the United Nations on 25 September 1958. It was an occasion for Blair to introduce university officials President Hannah, treasurer Philip May, and James Denison to his friends from the world of

Lyle Blair (l), R. K. Narayan, and Anthony West of the *New Yorker* at the Algonquin Hotel reception for *The Guide*, 1958

publishing and government. The invitees to this grand affair, in addition to U. Thant, the secretary general of the United Nations, and Henry Cabot Lodge, the American ambassador, included some prominent writers and editors. Harvey Breit, the *New York Times* columnist, and Leon Edel, the Henry James biographer, attended. Among the editors present were John Fisher of *Harpers*, William Shawn of the *New Yorker*, Charles Rollo of the *Atlantic Monthly*, and Norman Cousins of the *Saturday Review*. Two obscure government officials, George V. Allen and Joseph Privatera of the United States Information Agency, were also invited and presumably attended. Mr. Privatera would eventually complicate, compromise, and imperil Blair's friendship with his most notable author, R. K. Narayan.

THE JOY OF PUBLISHING: LETTERS TO EMILY 1954–58

Emily Schossberger, the director of the University of Nebraska Press (and later the director of Notre Dame's press), was a dear friend of Blair's. She was also a colleague, a crony, a co-conspirator, and, in some sense, a student. Blair's letters to Emily contain a good deal of philosophizing about university press publishing; detailed advice about budgeting, printing, and sales; and, above all, insights into Blair's early days as director. The letters, extending from 1954 until Emily's death in 1979, are a more personal and candid version of the monthly reports he was no longer required to write.

Blair's practical advice about advertisements and printers constituted what is now called "mentoring" and "networking," two terms Blair would surely have despised and spurned in favor of gossip, scheming, or fixing. Blair wrote, for example, that he was doing a book review program on MSU's station WKAR-TV "to an estimated audience of three women and a dog," and assured Emily that he was always ready to "plug" one of her books or "plant" a review. On 26 May 1954, shortly after MSU's Dean Edward Hardin accepted the post of provost at the University of Nebraska, Blair wrote Emily a reassuring note about his educational efforts with Hardin: "I am taking Dean Hardin to lunch and will do what I can, but you will rest assured that he will cast a friendly eye on the Press."

Blair's luncheon seminar with Dean Hardin was but one expression of his concern for the education of administrators. In another letter he elaborated on the press director's high-level instructional responsibilities. In a 25 March 1954, letter, Blair arranged to meet Emily for lunch during an Association of American University Presses conference. Blair scorned the afternoon sessions on "production problems," or "problems of the small press." "I suppose it sounds arrogant," he wrote, "but we really do not have any problems, and I suspect that the reason for this is that we have a decent administration who allow us to go our own way without let or hindrance." The cordial relations with his administration, Blair went on to explain, were the result of his educational efforts: "I suspect that many of the presses run into trouble because they do not educate their administration and keep them educated. My first year here presented my biggest problem, and that was teaching everyone from the President to the Comptroller something about publishing, and now that they know a little about it, I can only say, that they give us generous and sympathetic help."

The following year, on 25 March 1955, Blair responded to some specific questions from Emily, clarifying his position as director of the Press and chairman of the Board of Directors. "The press," he wrote, "is a separate corporation, buys where it chooses, spends what it chooses and publishes what it hopes are good books." His Board of Directors, Blair continued, "operates in a manner which can be called neither supervisory, policy making, nor executive. It is composed of individuals of each

School, appointed by the President." The board voted on every manuscript the Press accepted and every vote, Blair boasted, had been unanimous during his tenure. The board was "a group of individuals who might be termed 'friends of the Press.'" His budget, he explained, was "mainly a sort of intellectual guessing game of how we will make out for the year." The Press was "a non profit corporation separate from—but partially dependent on the college." The partial dependence was no problem in 1955. Blair seemed satisfied with "free light, heat, and rent, plus a subsidy of $14,000 a year."

Blair at that time neither had nor desired faculty status. As he explained to Schossberger, "I quite deliberately am not a faculty member although I can be one any day I say the word. I find it advantageous to stand aside from faculty groups, using it as an excuse not to sign petitions and join organizations, the fact that I am not a member of the faculty."

Blair at this point enjoyed a good working relationship with the university administration: "The administration has every confidence in me and I have every confidence in them. We make it a point to see that everyone knows what we are doing." The Press's freedom and independence was admired, envied, and disbelieved. He had tried to explain the Press's independence to other press directors at AAUP conferences, "and I know in their minds they have regarded me as a damn liar."

Blair's enthusiastic letters to Emily Schossberger communicate something of his joy of publishing or at least a high degree of job satisfaction. Relations with the administration were ideal and, above all, the books were exciting. In several letters Blair shared his excitement about books and authors. He rejoiced over the sales of J. O. Veatch's *Soils and Land of Michigan* and boasted that the entire first edition would be sold. "We will lose a mere $5,000," he wrote, and went on to explain that the book would provide a service to the state of Michigan that "could not be bought for $400,000." Another book, *The Soviet Penetration of Sinkiang*, had a colorful coauthor, "an ex-Chinese Communist general now resident on Formosa." Blair observed that "he is really a delightful thug and quite as bad as any Russian, except for the fact that he is quite open about it. At one time or another he made a deal, to his own advantage, with Chiang Kai-shek and now lives under the generalissimo's patronage."

Although he boasted to other press directors about his independence, Blair knew that this independence was not unlimited. He was a realist with an exquisite sense of the suitable. Thus in 1953 he discouraged, graciously but firmly, a fellow Australian who wanted to publish a book about American soldiers in Korea. In a letter to MacMayhon Ball, professor of

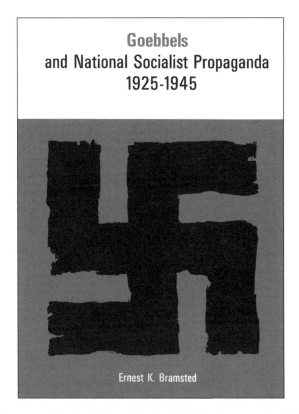

Ernest K. Bramstead's *Goebbels and National Socialist Propaganda 1925-1945* (1965)

political science at the University of Melbourne, Blair explained the necessary prudence of the academic publisher: "We are a state supported university. All our funds are voted to us annually by the State legislature and, as we were a predominantly rural state this legislature is not surprisingly a conservative body. Therefore, we have to take care that the books we publish are books of a noncontroversial nature in relation to religion or politics. I do not mean by this that there is any sort of censorship, but since I came here I have, for the reasons I have outlined above, vigorously opposed publishing books from either the extreme right or the extreme left. We have, moreover, published a book entitled *Midwestern Progressive Politics*, so you can see that we do not carry this policy to ridiculous conclusions."

In addition to these general, self-imposed restrictions, Blair explained the special circumstances of the Press during John Hannah's period of public service:

> There is also a second consideration. The President of the University is, at the moment, a member of General Eisenhower's Cabinet, and is directly responsible for the manpower problems of the U.S. Armed Forces. As a matter of good taste, we would, whilst Mr. Hannah holds this position, be unwilling to publish a book which reflected on the behavior of the United States occupational troops and, therefore, be an implied criticism of our President—published, as it were, behind his back.

Blair graciously offered to help Professor Ball find another publisher and concluded his letter with this wry, self-amused tribute to the tolerance of MSU and the Midwest:

> I have a sneaking suspicion that all Universities have these problems and that, therefore, you will understand them very readily. I would like to add that ours is a most understanding body. After all, here I am, an Australian citizen, camped down in the Middle West, of mildly unconventional habits and a positive genius for getting into accidents. Nevertheless, I have never worked in a more completely happy and cooperative atmosphere in my life.

PORTRAIT OF THE ARTIST AS PUBLISHER

Like many other great editors, Lyle Blair was not himself a prolific writer. He officially coauthored but two books; the curious, incomprehensible *Ashes to Ashes* with Rex Warner, and then in 1955 a brief, boiled-down thirty-nine-page version of Madison Kuhn's *Centennial History of Michigan State University*. Blair obviously did the writing for this souvenir-size history. His stylistic fingerprints—periodic sentences and archaic words like "whilst"—appear on every page.

Although he wrote few books himself, Blair was a very aggressive editor who made significant and invariably wise changes in his authors' works, as we have seen. Dissatisfied with Indian novelist R. K. Narayan's title *The English Instructor*, which to him sounded like a dreary educational tract, Blair changed the title for American readers to *Grateful to Life and Death*, the concluding line of the novel. When Ernest Bramstead published his classic study of propaganda, *Goebbels and National Socialist Propaganda 1925–1945*, he profited from Blair's editorial ear. The original title, *The Magic of Persuasion*, made Nazi propaganda seem inspiring or, as Blair put it, "sounds something like a tract from Billy Graham."

In addition to retitling books, Blair often encouraged the creation of books that would never have been written without his invasive intervention and inspiration.[5] He was increasingly outraged by American education, partly because his own children were attending East Lansing schools. The practice of "chewing gum days," when children were not only allowed, but encouraged to chew gum in school was sufficiently irritating to inspire schemes for a book-length protest. On 4 April 1958, Blair wrote his friend Marshall Best, vice president of Viking Publishers, about his plans to coauthor, with John Clark of the MSU English department, a critique of American education. Blair assured Best that the book would not be exaggerated in its criticism. He even acknowledged that the chewing gum scandals might not occur in every American school. He insisted, however, that "the fact that this can happen in a university town seems to us to indicate how thoroughly the colleges of education have emasculated certain school systems."

Blair's exposé of American education, "Alas, Poor Peter," apparently never got beyond the title page; nor did his plan to write a more ambitious, "comparative study of Australian/American education." In fact, Blair's concern for American education did not find expression until he imported an English friend, John Wales, to write *Schools for Democracy*. The making of this book is a good example of Blair's uncanny ability to envision a book, recreate his enthusiasm in an author, and then manipulate author and institution until the book was in print. Blair can be seen here as an extremely aggressive editor who, in some cases, became in fact, if not on title page, a coauthor.

John Wales was working for a British educational foundation when Blair approached him about writing a book on American education. His initial reaction to his old friend's suggestion was to plead incompetence. "What bothers me," he wrote in a 1 March 1960 letter to Blair, "is that, on any realistic view, I am completely unqualified to make this kind of study. It is true that I have been connected with education for the last thirty odd (some very odd) years, but it has been in a very specialized and unrepresentative way. I am no educationalist, in the American sense, and the professional jargon of the training college and the psycho-philosophical expert nauseates me as much as I am sure it does you."

Wales's disclaimers no doubt enhanced his credentials with Blair, who quickly arranged a temporary appointment for Wales at the Press and, of all places, the MSU School of Education. Now he could offer his reluctant author "a fee of $5,000, plus travel expenses." He also arranged to import another old friend from England, D. W. Brogan of Cambridge University.

Brogan joined the Blair household for a time while he wrote the introduction to *Schools for Democracy.*

John Wales's "research" during his extended reunion with Blair and
Brogan involved the construction of a "general knowledge" test, "to be set
to eighth and ninth graders." Some of these questions were—and are—
challenging:

> What is the meaning of the following and with what countries are they asso-
> ciated?
>
> > sphinx
> >
> > Centaur
> >
> > troll
> >
> > ideogram
> >
> > hieroglyph
> >
> > cuneiform

Wales also undertook to teach several junior high school classes what
they would have been learning in a typical British school. Students who
were used to discussing such life adjustment topics as "driver's licenses
should be issued to fourteen-year-olds" were treated to a scholarly lecture
on poetic imagery in Houseman and Milton.

Schools for Democracy was meant to be provocative, and its sharper points
seem to reflect Blair's views. His loathing of both Soviet Communism and
American education finds expression here. The argument that American
education was essentially totalitarian equalitarianism closer in ideology to
Kruschev than to Jefferson has that special sting so characteristic of Blair's
prose.

Blair promoted *Schools for Democracy* as aggressively as he had arranged
it, but he soon pronounced it a "resounding failure." It had sold only
three hundred copies. He complained to Admiral Hyman Rickover:
"Sometimes I feel that the products of the Colleges of Education are
determined that they will never read any form of constructive criticism."

Rickover, America's most outspoken critic of education, replied that he
had already read the book and was "sick at heart that educational offi-
cialdom had been able to kill it with silence." In his next book, *American
Education—A National Failure* (Dutton, 1963), Rickover quoted Blair's letter and eleven pages from *Schools for Democracy.* In 1962 *The American
Scholar,* the journal of Phi Beta Kappa, selected Wales's book as "an out-

standing university press book." Thus Lyle Blair, irritated by East Lansing's "chewing gum day," was able to thrust MSU into the national post-Sputnik debate on education.

Although Blair regarded anthologies as "the lowest form of literary work," his 1957 edition of the *Selected Works of Henry Lawson* is an admirable tribute to a gifted but neglected Australian. Lawson was a late nineteenth-century writer whose ballads would earn for him what Blair called "the hideous and inaccurate title of Australia's National Poet." The short stories selected for this volume have real artistic merit and they preserve the Australia of the ninteenth century. Blair's introduction, moreover, is a revealing, indirectly autobiographical essay. It suggests something of the origin of Blair's complex identity and the major themes of his career as a publisher. Australia, "a dry and lonely land," appears in this brief introduction as an embittered poor relation, admiring and at the same time resentful of both England and America. America and England, Blair argued, both helped "to castrate Australian publishing"—the Americans by allowing English publishers to buy the Australian, as well as the American, rights to books and the British by using Australia as a "dumping ground for their colonial editions."

Australian publishers, without access to American markets, were unable to nourish a national literature. One result, Blair observed, was that "many a young Australian writer or editor has been forced to emigrate, and the export of brains has become a notable Australian characteristic." Blair's exile in America involved pain, loss, and anger. In a 1965 letter to James McCuley, the Australian poet and scholar, Blair referred to his "dream of coming back to Australia . . . to wage a long and prolonged fight to break this system."

Blair's experience as a colonial appears to have made him extraordinarily sensitive to neglected and obscure writers who worked in the shadow of established British achievements. He pursued and promoted such writers in Australia, Canada, and India. Throughout his career as an editor, Blair seemed to specialize in literature united in language, literature written in "our common tongue." It was this interest in colonial or commonwealth literature that gave him and the MSU Press a distinctive identity. In the process of forging that identity Blair had many occasions to demonstrate the virtues he attributed to Henry Lawson—"fire in his belly and compassion in his heart."

This compassion is evident in a 1955 letter concerning the Lawson edition. "If Mrs. Lawson," he wrote to Australian publisher George Mackaness, "is in reduced circumstances, I will be more than happy to assign my royalties to her." Later, when his friend Emily Schossberger "got herself tangled up with a lawn mower," he urged fellow Association of American University Press members to send her letters. When James Denison was dying in 1975, Blair wrote former Press employees now scattered around the country urging them to write letters.

Blair's "fire in the belly" is evident in both his enthusiasm for books and his refusal to make peace with human stupidity. The fire was sometimes stoked to a towering inferno of rage by relatively minor matters. For example, he seemed to have a difficult time adjusting to Midwestern folksiness and back-slapping familiarity. In 1976—after twenty-four years at Michigan State University—he went into culture shock when confronted with the insolent familiarity of an insurance agent whose letter addressed him as "Lyle." Blair's response to this outrage was to fire off an angry letter to the general manager of the Massachusetts Mutual Life Insurance Company.

> Dear Sir:
>
> Enclosed herewith is a classic example of Alienation. Your agent has the audacity to address me by my first name without any type of formal introduction. Furthermore, he has the singular impertinence to comment on my work in the University of which he is totally ignorant.
>
> I would never do business with such a man and I suggest if you are going to retain his services you subject him to an intensive retraining program.

For the most part, Blair's outbursts were triggered by more serious matters; they had "objective correlatives," real values worth defending or real insults worth avenging. Always a counterpuncher, Blair never initiated a battle, but he never backed down from one either. His letters, he once admitted, often lacked a certain "conciliatory platitudinosity," especially when he was dealing with angry authors or hostile reviewers.

Lyle Blair generally got along with his authors. Many, of course, were old friends and many others quickly became new friends. Some authors, however, had totally unrealistic expectations about publication schedules, royalties, reviews, and complimentary copies. In 1956, Harvard professor William Elliot, the author of *Television's Impact on American Culture*, went over Blair's head and complained directly to President Hannah about getting galley proofs for the Japanese edition of his book. Blair in his response supplied the Japanese publisher's address, "in order that you may worry the person directly concerned." His concluding comment, a masterpiece of icy one-upsmanship, recalled an old ally who had made good. "Indeed the whole thing reminds me of a statement made to me over lunch by a colleague of mine, Harold MacMillan—temporarily absent from the publishing scene—"'Isn't it strange how authors, once we have risked our money in their books, think we stop reviewers from reviewing them, booksellers from selling them, and the public from reading them.'"

When angry authors barked at Blair he barked back; when they barked at his staff he could bite. One author who was bitten had sent an angry letter to Blair's assistant Jean Busfield and thereby violated Blair's standard of courtesy and professionalism. His response was blunt: "The amount of money you have cost us, the delays in publication date and your casual wanderings around the world, so that we could not work with you in any manner have been unspeakable. That you would dare under the circumstances write one of my staff a letter such as this speaks little of your ability of self-appraisal."

The next day Blair sent a copy of this letter to Jack Gallagher, now an editor at St. Martin's Press. In a cover letter he explained his uncharacteristic mildness: "Had I not written the old bag on the Sabbath my letter would have been even more appropriately unchristian."

Although he had a few squabbles with his authors, Blair more typically fought for, rather than with, his writers. His announced policy was never "to tilt with reviewers," but an unfair or misleading review could always inspire a sharp letter. One editor, whose reviewer had questioned the high price of a book, was informed that "your reviewer is totally ignorant of the economics of publishing." The suggestion that students would be required to purchase an overpriced book was also wrong and "an apology is called for."

Another book unfairly abused by a reviewer was Russel Nye's *This Almost Chosen People: Essays in the History of American Ideas*, published in 1966. The third Nye book to be published by the Press, *This Almost Chosen People* was dedicated to John Hannah and aimed at a general audience of educated readers who had a casual but by no means professional interest in American history.

By 1966 certain American ideas had brought the nation to the tragedy of Vietnam. Ideas about free enterprise, equality, or progress could no longer be contemplated with scholarly objectivity. That Nye quoted President Lyndon Johnson on the American sense of mission might in those days have been a provocation.

Whether it was the book's intrinsic imperfections or the era's discontents, *This Almost Chosen People* received some disturbingly negative reviews. Vague complaints about Nye's lack of originality had been muted in past reviews, small qualifications in otherwise positive evaluations. These complaints now found devastating expression in evaluations that were worse than negative. They were hostile, almost abusive attacks on the book and the author. Established reputations, in those days, were frequently assumed to be inflated. American ideas, moreover, were viewed with deep distrust.

Professor Richard Brion Davis of Cornell University wrote the harshest critique in the 3 September 1966 *Saturday Review*. Davis assailed the collection of essays as "oversimplified," "stale and platitudinous," and above all, insufficiently multidisciplinary. "Nye," David continued, "fails to confront the baffling, theoretical, methodological problem of intellectual history." His book, as a result, lacked "quantitative analysis," and "a firm theoretic framework."

Davis found the book's organization weak and its quotations repetitious and unselective. "One tires," Davis wrote, "of the same witnesses being recalled to say virtually the same thing." The content, moreover, was so elementary and basic that Davis questioned the book's intended audience. "So much space is devoted to summarizing basic American history that one almost has the impression of a series of lectures designed for a foreign audience."

To Professor Davis, *This Almost Chosen People* was not just a bad book, but a disgrace and, to judge by his language, a crime. Because of Nye's prestige, these essays could bring an entire discipline into disrepute. "Such a bad book," Davis concluded, "would not implicate an entire field of study if the author was not a highly knowledgeable and versatile historian."

Lyle Blair's response to the *Saturday Review*'s highly negative review was to run a full-page, upside down advertisement in the 6 October 1966 issue of the *New York Review of Books*.

At the bottom of the page and printed upside down was the comment, "We don't really take an upside-down point of view. We simply think this is a very fine book."

Blair's advertising counterattack against Professor Richard Brion Davis continued in the 20 October issue with another full-page ad recommending a positive review of Nye's book: "If you do like intellectual history, read the *Library Journal*, 15 September, 1966, p. 4132. A review of *This Almost Chosen People: Essays in the History of American Ideas* by Russel B. Nye." The upside down part of this ad offered a biblical explanation for Blair's feelings: "A soft answer turneth away wrath: but grievous words stir up anger."

If you don't like
intellectual history

read the Saturday Review
September 3, 1966, page 26
a review of
This Almost Chosen People:
Essays in
the History of American Ideas
by Russel B. Nye*

**Michigan State University Press
East Lansing**

.ʞooq ǝuɟ ʎɹǝʌ ɐ sı sıɥʇ ʞuıɥʇ ʎldɯıs ǝM
.ʍǝıʌ ɟo ʇuıod uʍop-ǝpısdn uɐ ǝʞɐʇ ʎllɐǝɹ ʇ,uop ǝM
*

What Blair called "our frivolous little ad" struck another reviewer, William Ward, as "coy." Ward, writing in the *American Historical Review*, praised *The Almost Chosen People* and gave the negative reviewer a mild scholarly slap. It was, Ward concluded, difficult "to believe that any American historian would not welcome the work of a professional who has chosen to turn to a greater audience."

Blair's ad may have dismayed some professional historians, but on 22 June he could gloat to an editor of the *Saturday Review*. "I can attest to the selling power of the *Saturday Review*. Largely due to the devastating attack on *The Almost Chosen People* in the *Saturday Review* we have sold out our first edition and have just ordered a rush reprint. No book on our list has ever sold better."

For all his "tilting with reviewers," Blair's most noteworthy battle was over a children's book published in 1957, and his adversary in this case was a librarian. The book, *The Wizard of Oz and Who He Was*, offered a scholarly, footnoted edition of the children's classic. Russel Nye contributed "An Appreciation" to the new edition and Martin Gardner, with

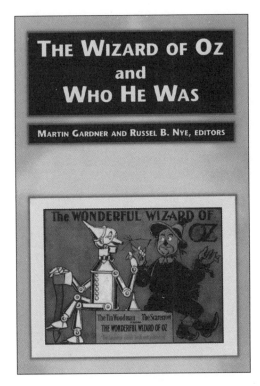

The Wizard of Oz and Who He Was (1957)

the help of L. Frank Baum's elderly widow, provided a short biography.[6] The MSU edition, a beautiful book with the original illustrations of W. W. Denslow, might have had a modest sale among dedicated Oz fanatics. The new edition found, however, a much larger audience after the director of Detroit libraries, Ralph Ulveling, charged that the book had a subversive effect on young minds.

Ulveling, attending a conference at the Kellogg Center in East Lansing, characterized the Oz books as "negative." His library didn't stock the books because "they drag young minds down to a cowardly level." The next day, *Lansing State Journal* reporter Neil Hunter featured Ulveling's remarks in an article entitled "Librarian Raps Oz Books."

What happened next is best told by Lyle Blair, in a 28 May 1957 letter to Anthony Boucher, the editor of *Fantasy and Science Fiction.*

One evening I returned from campus and my wife handed me the evening paper. In it was contained Ulveling's outburst. I was surprised and shocked.

Everybody in the book trade knew that we were producing *The Wizard of Oz and Who He Was*, and I imagine that most librarians knew this also. Certainly, Mr. Ulveling did, because I told him of my project well over a year ago. It seemed very odd to me that a guest on this campus would behave in such a manner, for I was unable to interpret it as anything but a deliberate slap at the editorial policies of this press. I had no knowledge that he was going to be interviewed, and had nothing to do with any form of plot for publicity purposes.

However, I did feel that such nonsense could not be left unanswered. I made an answer in the local press, and this was carried by the A.P. Wire Service, and the thing snowballed.

Blair's "answer to the local press" on 5 April explained the need for a new edition of the Baum classic. "It was because of this deep-seated dislike amongst certain librarians for the *Wizard of Oz* that The Michigan State University Press decided that the time had come for a critical appraisal of *The Wizard of Oz* and L. Frank Baum." After adding that "no one on the *creative* side of literature shares Mr. Ulveling's feelings," Blair presented a statement by Russel Nye.

Mr. Gardner and I said all that needs to be said about the strengths and weaknesses of the Oz books in our introduction to *The Wizard*. I am sure that Mr. Ulveling is as entitled to this opinion about them as are several million people who have only happy memories of the Land of Oz. If the message of the Oz books—that love and kindness make the world a better place—seems to be, as Mr. Ulveling says, of "no value" today, perhaps we need to reassess a good many other things about our modern society besides the Detroit Library's approved list of children's books.

Immediately after the press conference Blair went to work, alerting his friends in the publishing world and firing up the rage of civil libertarians who had endured the McCarthy years of fear and suspicion. Because of Blair's efforts a university press's scholarly edition of a children's book ignited a bitter conflict of more than local interest.

On the very day Blair and Nye issued their statement, Jim Vinall defended the *Wizard* in his radio broadcast on WJR in Detroit. After referring to rumors that books were being banned in Detroit, Vinall quoted Ulveling's characterization of the books as "negative," and went on to put the librarian's criticism in the context of the times. "Of course this is the era of the positive approach to everyone's thinking, life, eating, sleeping, rising, and even (in so far as possible) dying."

On April 16—just eleven days after Blair's press conference—Martin Gardner wrote Blair:

> What a wonderfully amusing ruckus you've kicked up in Detroit! One couldn't ask for better advance publicity—especially if it spreads to other cities. Is there any way the N. Y. C. library could be prodded into similar statements? Herb Alexander had told me that you were a master strategist at maneuvering things like this, and I watch with wonder while you pull the strings. Could it be that the book will really sell? Many thanks for keeping me informed and for the copies of the book. It is a handsome volume and I am proud to have my name on it.

Although Blair would later deny orchestrating the national protest against censorship, his response to Gardner's letter, written in the crisp tones of the battlefield communiqué, reported on the progress of the "ruckus."

> Last Saturday I recorded an interview for Monitor to be used some time this coming weekend. Last night I did another fifteen-minute broadcast on the subject, and later this week I will record another fifteen minute broadcast for a Detroit station. I have sent clips of the controversy to every major reviewing medium in the country, to say nothing of the *Library Journal* and the *Psychology Quarterly*. I think we are stirring up quite a controversy and a great deal of comment. In addition we have sent out over two hundred copies for review purposes.

Russel Nye soon tired of the controversy, but Blair held yet another press conference on 27 April and again lashed out at censors. The *Washington Post* printed his remarks. "At first they want to censor sex and keep young minds pure, but soon they move to politics, religion and other controversial areas." Even Blair's eight-year-old son David got into the act by staging a week long read-in for fifteen children at a campus bookstore. Blair's old friend Harvey Breit reported the news to readers of the *New York Times* and quoted the boy's characterization of censors as "psycho-ceramic."

Some notable national publications reported on the battle over a children's book. Even conservative publications such as *The Wall Street Journal* and *The National Review* came to the defense of the *Wizard.* Such periodicals had not been consistently critical of McCarthyism, but in defending

The Wizard of Oz they were able to enter a safe battle over an unambiguous issue with an easy enemy.

Martin Gardner eventually managed to "prod" some Florida librarians into making some more anti-Oz comments. The result was reported in his article, "The Librarians of Oz," which appeared in the 11 April issue of the *Saturday Review*. The librarians' officious moralizing invited comparison to the Oz character Professor H. M. Wogglebug, T. E. His initials, "Highly magnified," and his degree, "Thoroughly Educated," provided Gardner with the perfect symbol for those who would protect children from the delights of the *Wizard of Oz*.

Ralph Ulveling, the target of all this heavy artillery, launched a counterattack in the *American Library Bulletin*. The whole "alleged controversy," Ulveling claimed, was but a "publicity hoax." His library's policy was not to replace copies of the Oz books when they wore out. "This is not banning," he insisted, "it is selection."

Other librarians came to Ulveling's defense. Leroy Charles Merrit, professor of librarianship at the University of California (Berkeley) wrote Blair on 27 May "that it would seem that somebody has been confusing censorship with selection." He demanded to see the "direct quote from Mr. Ulveling which stirred both MSU and your publicity department to possibly take the name of censorship in vain."

Blair replied promptly and courteously to this letter, explaining how the "whole story just built up like Topsy and, naturally enough, we are glad it did."

Professor Merrit, responding on 3 June, accepted Blair's explanation, but added, "I still think you have done the library profession a disservice by so, oh so innocently, circulating to book review editors the stories accusing the Detroit librarian of censorship." Merrit concluded that Blair ought to be censured by the AAUP: "You are certainly guilty of trading, for a few pieces of silver, on the very real danger of censorship rampant in our country today." Blair, of course, launched another transcontinental missive to this "gratuitously insulting letter," but he eventually tired of his California pen pal and Merrit's next letter went unanswered.

Eight years later in 1965 Blair would recall in a letter to Bernard Perry, the director of the University of Indiana Press, that the Nye-Gardner edition of *Oz* received "more publicity than any other book we ever published," and from a financial standpoint was "one of the biggest flops we ever had." Only 1,642 copies had been sold by 1965.

In retrospect, the great wizard war of 1957 appears to have been about something more than censorship. It was, in a larger sense, about the general mood of the 1950s, an era of bland conformity, easy adjustment, and arrogant anti-intellectualism. To Lyle Blair the whole controversy must have seemed like yet another example of "alienation," the irritating familiarity of insurance salesmen, the outrage of "chewing gum days" in school. Blair's response to the Children's Library Association helps put the controversy—and the decade—in perspective:

> Personally, I think that the statement by the executive secretary of the Children's Library Association to the effect that *The Wizard of Oz* would not have been too bad if L. Frank Baum had had a good children's editor is rather like saying that if John Bunyan had had a good religious editor when he was writing *Pilgrim's Progress*, he would have come up with *The Power of Positive Thinking*.

Earning the "Subsidy"

The Press's relationships to university departments were both complex and tedious, with predictable opportunities for misunderstanding and conflict. The printing of syllabi, lab manuals, and professors' personalized textbooks was routine, uninspiring, and far removed from the more creative aspects of university publishing. Yet these services, as William Rutter had pointed out, were in effect the Press's subsidy, the meat and potatoes that made possible the more exotic items on the menu. To the departments, moreover, these were significant publications, jewels in some professor's bibliography, and the Press, like the old bookstore print shop, was expected to produce them efficiently and promptly. Given Blair's touchy sense of decorum and high professional standards, conflicts with the departments were inevitable.

One battle is especially notable because it is representative of faculty-press relations at their worst and because of the heavy artillery that was finally brought onto the battlefield.

In the spring of 1959 the Communication Skills Department strenuously objected to the Press's attempt to impose editorial standards on the communication skills syllabus. Blair was off in Australia at the start of this skirmish, but his aid Jack Gallagher promptly informed him of the impending hostilities:

> Engel from Comm Skills was in this morning. About ten percent of the revisions we suggested have been carried out; the other ninety percent have been rejected and the parts of the ms to which they referred remain

untouched. I explained to Engel that in this case nothing more could be done until you returned; I take it they don't want to wait. He again said who in hell were we to tell them what should go into the syllabus and again said if we wouldn't go along the dept. would have the thing done on its own.

Blair's first response was a telegraph to Gallagher: "Don't explode. Letter Follows." In the following letter Blair conceded that if Engel had said "who in hell were we to tell them what should go into the curriculum, I would quite agree with him." He insisted, however, that "we have every right, and will always maintain the right, to organize a text or syllabus in the best possible way when it appears under our imprint."

Jack Gallagher, while in New York on Press business, visited his friend Jacques Barzun, the dean of Columbia University's graduate school. Gallagher apparently discussed the comm skills matter with Barzun and gave him a copy of the disputed document. In any event, Barzun soon returned the proofs with delightfully malicious marginal comments. Few students are able to talk back to a syllabus, but Columbia's distinguished dean left devastating comments concerning the content, the logic, and, above all, the language of the hapless document. A great mind meeting a hopeless muddle made for some comedy worth recording.

The syllabus section headed "American Poet as Spokesman" might seem innocent enough to an MSU freshman, but Barzun asked, "For what, and what else could he be?" Another group of readings categorized as "Industrial Civilization on Trial" prompted Barzun to bark back, "We haven't had the industrial civilization yet and suddenly it's on trial." Other ambiguous phrases, "The Heritage from the American Past," and "Sentimental Action," provoked an increasingly testy Barzun to ask, "What language is this?"; "What in God's name is this?"; and "Irish Bull."

The syllabus also offered some study skills advice that was even more laughable than its fractured version of American history. The question concerning a reference work, "What does it include and exclude," suggested an obvious answer to Barzun: "the contents of all other books." Finally, the Comm Skills Department's admonition to "avoid gross errors in diction," inspired Barzun's question, "Why not avoid them all?"

Barzun's final comment on the communication skills course was expressed in a 29 June letter to Gallagher: "My opinion confirms yours; the intention and the readings are good; the execution is poor. Logic, history, and good prose are by turns ignored, and something very like the model of an average mind is exhibited for the student's imitation."

Barzun's letter arrived after an editorial meeting had resolved the issue, and Gallagher and Blair never had to confront their adversaries with Barzun's judgments. The episode suggests, nevertheless, the kind of challenge the Press's "subsidy" entailed. Lyle Blair had little tolerance for the "average mind," and he had no intention of being a mere printer, fulfilling orders of faculty members whose literary standards were unacceptable.

THE PUBLISHER AS PROFESSOR

In 1955 Blair had assured Emily Schossberger that he could join the faculty as full professor any time he wanted. By 1975 things had changed and the director of the Press, like other faculty, had to campaign for promotion. For this distasteful task Blair assembled an *apologia pro vita summa* of documents and testimonials which give a sense of the publisher as a professor. As "Professor of Comparative Literature," he was probably the most distinctive and unusual professor to sport such a title since Ford Maddox Ford taught down the road at Olivet College. Blair, like Ford, seemed to impress students not so much by what he taught, but by what he was: a citizen of the world, an old-fashioned man of letters.[7]

Blair's teaching career consisted of only two courses. The first, offered in 1958, was an informal discussion group, located conveniently in the Press's Berkey Hall offices and titled "The Educated Man." By modern, politically correct standards this course might be viewed as an unapologetically elitist, eccentric, and casual examination of current events. In a letter recommending a student for a Rhodes Scholarship, Blair recalled the course and the student. "Actually," he wrote, "the weekly discussions will range from the consequences of the disintegration of the Ottoman Empire to the art of Picasso, from the ultimate consequences of rockets to a new novel by Graham Greene, from T. S. Eliot's new play to the validity of the American impressionists. In other words, anything which is of interest to the mind is examined." The subject of this letter had confided to Professor Blair his worry that he was not "a joiner or one of a merry group." To Blair such concerns were yet another indictment of American education: "That this should worry him is by no means surprising considering the pressures for conformity which exist in American society and in American university life today. Time," he concluded, "will teach him that the way of the intellectual can be nothing but lonely and this knowledge, in turn, will soften him."

In 1975 when he was campaigning for promotion to full professor, Blair offered another course titled "The Literature of the British

Commonwealth in the Twentieth Century." This course, obviously less casual and more traditionally literary than "The Educated Man," concerned "the curious interplay of cultures within the British Commonwealth." It examined "the influence of England on the literature of India, Australia, New Zealand, and South Africa, and the influence that those countries . . . exerted on the cultural life in England in return."

Blair's promotion package included some impressive recommendations. Russel Nye wrote about Blair's contributions to the Press and concluded that "the MSU Press over the years has established an unusually strong and distinguished list of books in literature and the humanities." Blair's peers in scholarly publishing tended to stress his unique combination of ordinarily incompatible skills. Robin Wilson, the associate director of the Committee on Institutional Cooperation, observed that "Like all press directors, Lyle has been forced to combine the instincts and values of the scholar with the pragmatic skills of the businessman." Few press directors, he continued, "select, edit, design, produce and sell books without a legion of specialists to help them. Lyle does."

Carroll Bowen, of Harvard University Press, was most impressed with Blair's courage and integrity. Several years before, he recalled, Blair had published a volume that turned out to be plagiarized. "He moved without hesitation to sacrifice his investment in the volume and scrapped the publication. I regarded his action then and now as the only possible course of action, but I am obliged to report that though other publishers have discovered plagiarism, not all have addressed themselves so rigorously to its eradication. For the scholarly tradition is a fragile one and without zealous and vigilant protection erodes. I regard the incident as exemplifying Lyle's personal and professional integrity." To Bowen, Blair's management of the Press constituted "one of the persisting miracles of small business entrepreneurship in an otherwise dismal university publishing scene."

Chapter 3

"A One-Man Operation"

The praise lavished on Lyle Blair by his university press peers Robin Williams and Caroll Bowen may have been more accurate than they knew. Blair's pragmatic business skills, combined with his network of old friends, made for some "entrepreneurship" of astonishing boldness.

In the Cold War's Crucible

Blair's large network of World War II friends was not limited to old-fashioned men of letters who delighted in obscure literary classics. His mysterious background in Middle East intelligence provided another group of friends who saw books as weapons in the cold war against Communism. To these people the Michigan State University Press could become a useful producer of propaganda disguised as scholarship, another unit of the university willing to advance the aims of the American government.

The story of MSU's involvement in the tragedy of Vietnam has been told before, most dramatically in an article entitled "The University on the Make," which appeared in the April 1966 issue of *Ramparts* Magazine. In this issue, featuring a cover depicting Vietnam's Madam Nu as a cheerleader, Stanley K. Sheinbaum, a former MSU professor of economics, introduced his article with an autobiographical anecdote:

During the summer of 1958, I cut my vacation short and rushed off to San Francisco to meet the four leading police figures of South Vietnam. Among them they controlled the Saigon police, the national police and the VBI, South Vietnam's equivalent of the FBI.

Within an hour of their arrival the youngest, a nephew of Ngo Dinh Diem, conspiratorially drew me aside and informed me that one of the others was going to kill the eldest of the group. The story he told possessed plot and counter-plot. In essence, Michigan State University was being used to invite these men to the United States under the auspices of its foreign aid

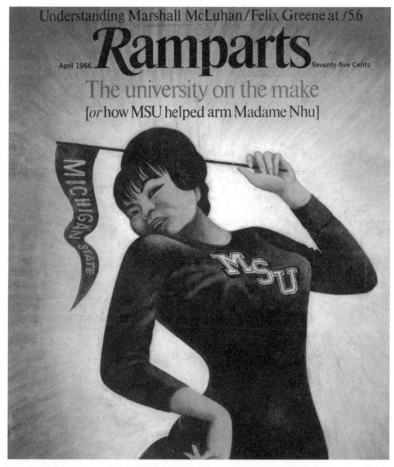

Understanding Marshall McLuhan/Felix Greene at ƒ5.6

Ramparts

April 1966   Seventy-five Cents

The university on the make
[*or* how MSU helped arm Madame Nhu]

Ramparts **Magazine, April 1966 (illustration courtesy of Paul Davis Studios).**

contract in Vietnam. The dirty deed was to be done prophylactically in the States, uncluttered by any complicating factors in Saigon.

The execution was postponed until the group returned to Vietnam, but the story served, nonetheless, as a sensational introduction to Sheinbaum's account of MSU's adventure in foreign affairs. Diem, in exile, had been befriended by Wesley Fishel, an MSU professor searching for a scholarly project, some "evidence of merit" for his annual report. When he returned to power in Vietnam, Diem had an honorary MSU degree and access to the resources of a university. Fishel and other faculty members went off like county extension agents to lend their expertise to the task of nation building. Providing knowledge in the land-grant spirit of service was not new, of course, but this project, Sheinbaum argued, was clandestine and corrupting.

The university, Ramparts alleged, had been penetrated by the CIA, and the more worldly departments, Political Science and Police Administration, had acquiesced in faculty appointments for CIA operatives. The CIA men, it was rumored in Saigon, could be distinguished from the real professors because they spoke better French.

Although James Denison was identified as one of four faculty members who were sent to Vietnam as an "inspection team" to consider Diem's request for aid, the Michigan State University Press was not mentioned in the *Ramparts* article—or in subsequent studies of MSU's Vietnam project. Materials in the Press archives indicate, however, that various government agencies, including the United States Information Agency (USIA), Agency for International Development (AID), and Institutional Cooperation Administration (ICA), secretly contributed to a variety of publications. There is no mention of the CIA in this alphabet of agencies, but the ultimate source of these secret funds is highly suspect.

Blair's involvement with government organization apparently began as soon as he arrived on campus. As early as 12 May 1953, he planned to publish a book called "Atrocity," a study of Communist propaganda written by Wesley Fishel and Herbert Garfinckle. The book's subtitle, recorded in Blair's report to the Press board, gives a more detailed description: "a study of Russian, Chinese, and North Korean atrocity propaganda directed against the United States and her Allies during the course of the Korean War."

When *Look* magazine editor Margery Darnell inquired about publishing chapters of this book as magazine articles Blair replied that publication would be delayed, "for reasons that are very hush hush in the realms of security." Later he explained to Ms. Darnell that "the State Department, together with the Army, has failed to clear all the material."

"Atrocity" was never published by Michigan State University Press, but the following year Blair arranged for financing of his old friend R. G. Casey's book, *Friends and Neighbors.* Casey, because of his appearance and his achievements, was known as "the Anthony Eden of Australia." He had been governor of the Indian province of Bengal, ambassador to Washington, Australian Foreign Affairs secretary, and he would eventually (1965–69) become governor-general of Australia. Somewhere along the line, probably in India, he had met Blair, who, years later, was delighted to publish his book and arrange an honorary Doctor of Laws degree from

MSU in 1958. Casey's commencement address, published in the *Centennial Review*,[1] paid tribute to the Press's central role in the university's international service. "I know," Casey said, "that the Michigan State University Press publishes works by others as well as Americans and Australians—Koreans, Chinese, Indians, Vietnamese, and others. These publications have helped to make widely known in many countries of the world your very considerable international research and your overseas technical assistance projects." The book's publication was celebrated at the United Nations, where various dignitaries, including the American delegate Henry Cabot Lodge, gathered around Blair to pose for photographs with copies of *Friends and Neighbors*.

Government support of Casey's memoir was both generous and secretive. USIA agreed to pay $7,026.00 for "publication and overseas distribution" of a paperback edition. They also contracted to buy 25,000 copies of *Friends and Neighbors* for $5,167.50. This aid was given in strict secrecy, for the contract with the Press stipulated that "the contractor will not issue, written or otherwise, or permit to be issued publicity in any form respecting the government's participation in the publication of said books."

The government's generosity to this book extended beyond publication costs and bulk sales. Three years later, on 8 July 1957, Blair, eager to convey more "pleasant news," wrote Casey that "via the U.S. State Department (this much is confidential), we are arranging for *Friends and Neighbors* to be translated into Chinese and published in Hong Kong. This edition will be circulated in Formosa and amongst all Chinese language communities in Southeast Asia. Furthermore, by devious means, a certain circulation will be achieved on the Chinese mainland." After discussing his own forthcoming trip to Australia (with stops in Singapore and Saigon) Blair again expressed his pleasure in the Chinese translation. "This is the first time," he concluded, "the United States government has supported such a project for a book written by anyone other than a U.S. citizen."

The Casey book, for all the secrecy, was little more than an elder statesman's memoir. A brief review in the *Nation* dismissed the volume as "generalities and the obvious." The *New York Times* characterized the book as "extraordinarily bland." It certainly contained nothing which would have ignited a rebellion in Communist China. Blair, however, took his covert activities seriously. On 8 February 1963, he sent Ernest Bramstead, the author of *Goebbels and National Socialist Propaganda*, a copy of the letter to Lord Casey, presumably the one quoted here concerning American propaganda aimed at the Chinese mainland. Blair warned him that the enclosed letter to Lord Casey was "for your very private and confidential information. Please destroy it as soon as you have read it."

Another MSU Press book that benefited from secret government subsidies was *Vietnam: The First Five Years: An International Symposium*, edited by Richard Lindholm, a former MSU professor and, in 1959, dean of the School of Business at the University of Oregon. This symposium on Vietnam was originally to be edited by Wesley Fishel, but at a Board of Directors' meeting on 10 December 1957, Richard Chapin and Gordon Sabine moved that the book not be published.

In 1959 *Vietnam: The First Five Years* turned up again, this time with Richard Lindholm as editor. The volume was a crudely assembled series of papers and responses designed to give the impression of a scholarly debate or a dialogue of disinterested, objective specialists. From its inception, *Vietnam: The First Five Years* was deformed by conflicts and contradictions. The initial call for contributors set the tone. Abandoning all pretense of scholarly objectivity, Lindholm's prospectus seemed to be recruiting cheerleaders rather than scholars. Participants were asked to present papers that would "make available the experience and opinions of Vietnamese and other citizens of the Free World who have been working hard during the past three years to make Vietnam a better place in which to practice the principles of individual religious beliefs, to raise a family, to develop freely a useful career, and to enjoy the comforts and standard of living that well managed technology can provide." South Vietnam, in Lindholm's grand suburban vision, sounded a lot like East Lansing, but the contributors to this project were not the usual bookish scholars.

General Edward Lansdale was a nearly mythic figure who had almost single-handedly "saved" the Philippines by helping his friend Ramon Magsaysay crush the Communist Huk Rebellion. His life had inspired Blair's old friend Graham Greene to base a central character on him in *The Quiet American*. He was also fictionalized in Eugene Burdick's *The Ugly American*. By 1960, Landsdale was advising President Kennedy on Vietnam. Other contributors to the volume included Bernard Fall, a journalist who turned against the war; Elon Hildreth, chief of the education division of United States Operations Mission in Saigon; Frederick Wickert, professor of psychology at MSU; and Blair's old friend R. G. Casey, the Australian minister for external affairs. Mary de Zouche was available to translate the French contributions.

In the course of assembling this peculiar book, Blair and Lindholm had plenty of warnings about the essential absurdity and questionable

Vietnam: The First Five Years: An International Symposium (1959)

honesty of the project. A number of government officials declined to participate and one, General Lansdale, agreed to be published only if it could be done anonymously. With his usual audacity, Blair wrote to Secretary of State John Foster Dulles. Dulles did not respond personally, but Assistant Secretary of State Walter S. Robinson expressed the secretary's reservations about the project in a 19 September 1957 letter to Blair:

> The Secretary of State has asked me to thank you for your kind invitation to him to contribute to your forthcoming book on Vietnam. He does not believe, however, that it would be appropriate for him as Secretary of State to participate in a public analysis of the affairs of an independent and sovereign nation, as such comment would be susceptible of misinterpretation within the country concerned.

Although grateful for the aid and support they have received from the free world, the Government and people of Vietnam feel that their progress since the Geneva armistice has been due largely to their endeavors. Accordingly, the Secretary would consider it more appropriate to have someone outside the United States government who is interested in Vietnamese affairs provide the views and analysis you request.

Dulles's views, as phrased by his aid, made a clear distinction between those officials who administer foreign policy and those scholars who analyze, evaluate, and, possibly, criticize it. An executive acts, the scholar analyzes, and to merge their distinctive roles, Dulles knew, would be both dangerous and deceptive.

Another, even more obvious, red flag appeared in a letter from an invited but eventually excluded contributor, Hilaire du Berrier. In a January 2 letter to Lindholm, du Berrier expressed some ominous reservations about the project:

> In anything that I have written in the past on South Vietnam I have kept constantly in mind the possibility that a year from now or two years from now a great upheaval is more than likely to take place in Southeast Asia. When that happens all the tongues that have been silenced to date will be able to speak and in the wave of Anti-American reaction that will follow no few Americans at home are going to find valid materials against the statesmen and educators and public relations agents who contributed to the forming of our policy."

Du Berrier concluded by warning that other contributors to the anthology might take care to write "innocuous passages," because of their doubts. Such cautious writing and thinking, he noted, "might raise the question of academic honesty in many minds."

By 20 June 1958, Wesley Fishel, General Edward Lansdale, and Lyle Blair were all alarmed by Du Berrier's involvement in the anthology. Blair's letter to Lindholm suggests the difficulties—editorial, political, and ethical—of assembling such a book:

> I have just had Fishel in here telling me that the State Department in general, and Edward Lansdale in particular, have been saying that you have been using Hilaire du Berrier as a reader for The Experiment in Vietnam. Furthermore, Fishel tells me du Berrier is a French spy or worse.

Now I remember this fellow did write something for you and, if my memory serves me correctly, it was bad. Mrs. Brothers is away and I cannot find it in the organization of the book. Has this been dropped? Anyway I wish you would give me a bit of a briefing on this, because Fishel says that Washington is talking about it. Presumably they are giving poor Glen Taggart an earful. If the man is a scoundrel we certainly should not have him in the book. Yet I am not quite sure that being a French spy brands him as a scoundrel. The French were engaged in a vicious war against Communist forces and they had to use whatever means they saw fit. Furthermore, Fishel always seems to me to be so bitterly anti-French that it distorts his general vision. He also tells me that Lansdale still seems to be under the opinion that the piece he wrote for you is going to be published. This is, of course, nonsense, and I think that you should write to him saying that Fishel has told me this to relieve his anxiety. [General Lansdale and du Berrier were both dropped from the book.]

Blair's reference to General Landsdale's opinion that he was going to be published refers to the general's desire to be published anonymously. Blair's emphatic "nonsense" is a tribute to his integrity in the midst of this very dubious enterprise. Blair's integrity, his core publisher's principles, were reiterated on 7 January 1966 when he replied to a Spanish publisher who wished to reprint Ernest Bramstad's *Goebbels and National Socialist Propaganda* in censored form:

I am afraid it is impossible to do business with you as it is against our principles to submit any scholarly work to any government for official censorship. This is a negation of scholarship which requires freedom more than anything else if it is to live.

The reviewers were openly skeptical about *Vietnam: The First Five Years,* and several seemed to detect the odor of propaganda. Hugh Tinker, a reviewer from the London School of Oriental and Asian Studies shared his concern with readers of *Pacific Affairs* in march of 1966. Tinker was astonished by the innocence of several contributors. "What are we to make of the following," he asked of one writer, a *Time-Life* correspondent who had written:

About 90 percent of the Vietnamese are illiterate. And illiteracy means much more than an inability to read and write; it also means a mind that functions at close to the five-year-old level, an utter absence of comprehension of even

the most basic political concepts, almost no capacity for logic. . . . Democracy
is an utter impossibility, a contradiction in terms, in a country that is 90 percent or even 50 percent illiterate.

Tinker went on to compare Vietnam with Pakistan, another country
supposedly saved by American aid and subsequently destroyed by corruption and the collapse into military dictatorship. He concluded his review
with a question, "Will South Vietnam in a year or two provide another
illustration of the nonsense of the saying that history never repeats itself?"

A Michigan State University professor named Robert G. Scigliano
expressed similar, almost identical reservations in his review for the
February 1960 issue of the *Journal of Asian Studies*. Scigliano noted the
confusion of the articles and commentaries; they seemed "carelessly
put together," but he quickly identified the fundamental flaw in the
project.

"Perhaps the basic problem is that many of them were written by individuals with personal or institutional commitments to the activities or projects they have written about. As a consequence, a certain blandness and
lack of objectivity toward one's own programs and a tendency to wrangle
over petty matters prevails in many parts of the collection."

Although Blair's principles remained uncompromised by government
subsidies, his editorial judgment sometimes failed him when tempted by
the irresistible combination of Australian author and anti-Communist
theme. There is no other explanation for the 1966 publication of W. G.
Goodard's *Formosa: A Study in Chinese History*. The reviews of this book
were unfavorable, almost abusive. The *American Historical Review*
denounced the book for its "dogmatic commentary and untenable thesis,
and numerous factual errors." The *Asian Student* pronounced it a "failure
as both history and interpretation."

On campus, Goddard's book inspired a faculty member to protest
both the book and the press that published it. On 2 June 1967, Bernard
Gallin, an associate professor of anthropology, sent an angry two-page letter to Louis McQuitty, the dean of social science. He included carbon
copies to President Hannah, Provost Howard Neville, and Moreau
Maxwell, chairman of the Department of Anthropology.

Professor Gallin's letter concerned "a most unpleasant and embarrassing experience" he had undergone at Columbia University when
confronted by angry anthropologists and China specialists. These
scholars demanded to know how the MSU Press could have published
a book "totally lacking in any semblance of scholarship," "filled with

inaccuracies," and "virtually devoid of any value."

After the humiliating confrontation in New York, Gallin returned to East Lansing and read Goodard's book about Formosa. "Shocked" by the lack of scholarship, he called a member of the Press's Board of Directors. The unidentified board member knew nothing about the book and said that the Press was "pretty much a one-man operation."

Gallin's letter also alleged, more generally, that the Press was "isolated from the academic community," and that the faculty shared his embarrassment. Michigan State University Press, he concluded, "has generally been a subject which faculty . . . prefer not to discuss—especially with outsiders."

Since Bernard Gallin's letter was written a year after the *Ramparts* exposé, it is possible that he and his Columbia University colleagues may have been predisposed to assume that inferior scholarship might be politicized scholarship. Dean McQuinty forwarded Gallin's letter to Provost Howard Neville and urged that the "entire matter be carefully studied," but nothing came of it. There is no record of Provost Neville ("Jake" to Blair) ordering any study. Possibly the university had no desire to reopen an old embarrassment at a time when both Vietnam and student protestors were volatile. Of course, the failure to respond to the Gallin letter might be but another example of an administrative tendency to ignore internal criticism while responding hysterically to external criticism. In any event, the "one-man operation" continued for thirteen more years.

Thus the Press during the Lyle Blair years developed a specialty of sorts in foreign policy studies. Some of these publications, such as Paul Varg's *Foreign Policies of the Founding Fathers* (1964) and *The Making of a Myth: The United States and China 1897–1912* (1968), were first-rate books that required no secret subsidies. In fact, it was not until 1966 that the Press again became entangled with the government's Cold War propaganda offensive.

As early as 4 November 1952, only six months after he arrived at the Press, Blair had envisioned or more likely enlisted in an ongoing project to develop and distribute inexpensive editions of American books in Asia. Minutes of the Board of Directors' meeting on that date record Press Director James Denison as reporting "the plan had been submitted by President Hannah to the Administration of the Point Four Program."

Blair, it should be noted, was exceedingly cautious, even deferential to Denison. When he had a unique opportunity to write a regular column about books for the *Nation* he worried about embarrassing the university. A 19 September 1953 letter to Denison expresses an odd combination of fear and desire:

> As you know, from our conversation this afternoon I have been invited to write a column on books and authors for the "Nation." I cannot stress too greatly that fact that the column will be confined purely to books and people associated with the book trade. Nevertheless, I do recognize that, as a State University, we have a particular duty to be above criticism, and should there be any dismay on the part of the College authorities over my writing for the "Nation," I am perfectly willing to abandon the project immediately. Naturally enough, I would be distressed because the book pages of the "Nation" are read throughout the country and I feel that the column will give us a certain prestige amongst book buyers and librarians everywhere.

Blair wrote one column for the *Nation*, some genial reflections about books, but a regular column never developed. In any event, his fear of disturbing the authorities makes it most unlikely that he would have undertaken any covert publishing projects on his own.

Fourteen years after the program was conceived Blair began to publish the "cheap books." The "cheap books" program, known more elegantly as the Mimosa editions, involved the distribution in Asia of foreign policy studies and American classics. By 1966, three months after the *Ramparts* article, the project was openly acknowledged as frankly propagandistic in purpose. *The State News*, in an article about Blair's world tour to promote the books, noted that the project was designed "to provide a new enthusiasm over the merits of Western thought and Western freedom and progress among nations endangered by the pressures of Soviet Russian Communism."

Although seven Mimosa books were intended, only three were actually published: *East and West Must Meet*, another "symposium" edited by Benjamin H. Brown; *Sinkiang—Pawn or Pivot*, by Allen Whiting and his "delightful thug" coauthor General Sheng Shihts; and Richard Henry Dana's *Two Years Before the Mast*, edited with an introduction by Russel Nye.

The Mimosa books were openly publicized as contributions to Cold War propaganda efforts; the only thing secret about the project was its financing. On 22 June 1966, the Board of Directors of the Press were informed that a special bank account had been opened in Sidney, Australia. The size of the account was never mentioned, but it was made clear that these funds were "in effect property of the United States government," and they could be disbursed only with checks

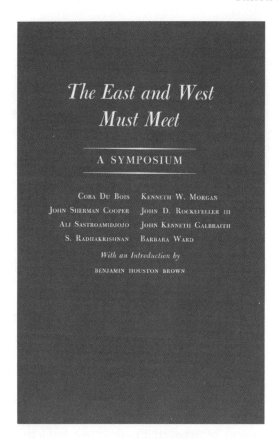

The East and West Must Meet, **Benjamin H. Brown, editor (1959)**

cosigned by treasurer Phillip May and Press director Lyle Blair.

Blair's involvement in secret government subsidies must be seen from both a historical and a personal perspective. Historically universities, like the aerospace industry, were major beneficiaries of the government's cold war spending. The expanding federal government pumped massive funding into university research, directly and indirectly subsidizing the education of millions of students.

Arthur Schlesinger Jr., in reflecting on his own anti-Communism, suggested that the liberal anti-Communism might be better understood if the word Communism was read as Stalinism. Once the distinction between Communism and Stalinism is made, Schlesinger's conclusion can be seen in the context of the times. "I can only say that I have not the slightest regret for the campaign my contemporaries waged against

Stalinism.[2]

MSU had from the very beginning been a public service institution; such, in fact, had been the purpose of Justin Morrill's land-grant legislation establishing state universities. In the 1950s the land-grant spirit of service was uncritically extended to the task of "nation building." Service to the State of Michigan could be easily expanded into service to the state of Vietnam.

The CIA, moreover, had sponsored a variety of intellectual enterprises throughout the cold war years. American and British intellectuals, including such luminaries as Irving Kristol, Stephen Spender, and Arthur Schlesinger Jr., had benefited from the CIA-supported Congress for Cultural Freedom. This front organization supported the distinguished British journal *Encounter* from 1953 to 1966. Although the *New York Times* exposure of CIA support for *Encounter* on 27 April 1966, set off a fratricidal war among intellectuals, it appears, in retrospect, that government money in this case empowered rather than corrupted.[3]

From a personal perspective, Lyle Blair, it should be remembered, was a zealous anti-Communist. In his 1955 "keepsake"-size history of MSU, Blair had juxtaposed Justin Morrill and Karl Marx in the year 1855. While the congressman was writing the Morrill Act, "Karl Marx was writing a book entitled *Das Capital,* a book destined for oblivion in the western world."

Blair's anti-Communism was no doubt shared by President Hannah. Blair often reported to President Hannah on his travels in Southeast Asia, and sometimes fired off letters of protest to Hannah about Communist speakers on campus. In a 17 February 1967 letter, Blair reminded Hannah that he had been silent the last time Dr. Han Suyin, "a pro-Peking propagandist," was on campus. Her second visit as a paid lecturer inspired yet another letter lacking in "conciliatory platitudinosity."

I now find to my horror that she has been invited here to participate in the Lecture Concert Series (for a considerable sum of money) and I feel that I must protest once more at our naiveté in subsidizing this woman's pro-Peking, anti-American line. If rumor has it right, not only are we paying her well but are giving her every opportunity to pursue her pernicious theme, which she does in the classical manner. On her previous visit we were told that she would educate the students. She didn't do much of a job of it. In reply to a question about the Red Guards, she described them as Boy Scouts

and if the Red Guards are Boy Scouts, then I am a character out of Little

Women."

It is not surprising, then, that Blair's anti-Communism, combined with his ambitions for his underfunded press, would encourage him to seek secret subsidies from the government. Given his views, Blair would not have experienced any cognitive dissonance of painfully clashing values. Fighting Communism while financing the Press and pleasing his board must have appeared to Blair as an exceedingly attractive triple play.

In seeking subsidies from secretive government agencies Blair may have contributed in a small way to the corruption of the university and the tragedy of Vietnam. From a personal and literary standpoint, however, the greatest harm came from risking his relationship with R. K. Narayan.

Narayan's 1956 trip to the United States had been a triumph for both the novelist and his publisher. It demonstrated, among other things, Blair's ability to bring an internationally renowned writer to campus. Narayan's 1958 trip to America was much less successful, at least from Lyle Blair's perspective. Narayan's *Dateless Diary* manuscript was in terrible shape and Marshall Best, the Viking Press editor, had expressed his reservations about publishing it. Blair, for his part, was prepared to do some aggressive, overbearing editing. He promised Narayan that he would "work with you on it," and "help you in sharpening your editorial eye."

In addition to *The Dateless Diary*, Blair wanted Narayan to write another book for the Mimosa series. This book would be a biography of the Philippine leader Ramon Magsaysay, who had recently been killed in a plane crash. Long before he had a manuscript or even a rough draft, Blair had a title, "Looking for Magsaysay," and a patron to subsidize the proposed biography.

In a 20 February 1958 letter to Joseph Privatera, the USIA's chief of book development, Blair expressed his pleasure in learning that the agency wanted Narayan to write a biography of Magsaysay. The Philippine leader had been an effective anti-Communist who had decisively defeated the leftist Huk rebels. General Edward Lansdale had been his chief advisor, and the victory over Communism in the Philippines was an acknowledged model for American efforts in Vietnam. "We," Blair wrote, would be willing to "commission" Narayan to write the book, but a grant of $2,500 would be needed "to cover editorial expenses" and the USIA would be expected to purchase 3,500 copies of the biography. Eight days later Donald McNeil, another executive in the publications activities branch, replied with a "Dear Lyle" letter offering a $2,500 advance, "upon receipt of an outline of the proposed book." Narayan, he assured Blair, would also receive "all possible assistance from our post in Manila." There was, however, one reservation about the subsidy: "There will be no indication on our part to Narayan that we are participating in the project."

In his 8 March 1958 response to McNeil, Blair agreed to the secret subsidy and the deception of Narayan. He also offered a more detailed description of the biography:

> The book is not to be a scholarly, precise, minute by minute biography. Rather it will tend to paint a portrait of Magsaysay as a man, as a husband, as a father, as a politician, and then as a unique national leader. The book will endeavor to bring out the enormous vitality and friendliness of the man and also to reflect faithfully through Magsaysay the fact little believed or accepted in Asia that, on the whole, the people of the Philippines are genuinely fond of and grateful to the United States.

Blair's concluding comment to McNeil described the dominant role he intended to play in the writing of the biography: "This is the outline I have given Narayan to work to; and it will be molded into shape under my direction when he visits the campus with his notes and starts to write the book. In the writing we will be working together from the first to the last page so that the outline you now possess is one that will be followed."

The outline, which appears in the government contract, is presumably the one Blair submitted. The contract also stipulates that "no attribution to the Agency will be indicated. . . ."

After the encouraging letter from the USIA Blair promptly wrote Narayan that he had been "chosen" to write the Magsaysay biography. Without mentioning the secret subsidy or its source, Blair offered his assistance:

> I can arrange to fly you from Mysore to Manila, to San Francisco, to Lansing, to New York, to Mysore provided that your living expenses do not exceed $2,500. In addition to this, should you come to Lansing, the University is willing to give you a suite in the Kellogg Center for the ten weeks whilst we work on the book, and an honorarium of $1,500 as a visiting distinguished professor in the College of Communication Arts.

Narayan's 1958 trip to Michigan State University, for all the strings Blair pulled, was a distressing failure. The Magsaysay biography was written but never published, Narayan got an extra $500 advance from the Press and then "eloped" with a typewriter he mistakenly thought had been given to him. The typewriter had to be uncrated in New York and shipped back to East Lansing. With much gnashing of teeth, Blair purchased another typewriter, shipped it to India, and then initiated a snarling correspondence with the College of Communication Arts concerning the typewriter, which had compromised "the honor of the university."

Blair's still seething frustrations with Narayan exploded over a year later in a 23 June 1961 letter to Helen Strauss, Narayan's agent at the William Morris Agency. After curtly summarizing all that had been done for Narayan, the advances and accommodations, even the typewriter, Blair raged against the Magsaysay manuscript which was "a most disgracefully sloppy piece of work."

The Magsaysay project appears to have damaged, if not ended, the close friendship and creative partnership between the novelist and the publisher. Narayan's next visit to the United States in 1962 did not include any visits to Michigan State University or any meetings with Lyle Blair. Blair's generous promotion of Narayan in the 1950s had made possible American recognition and literary fame. Ved Mehta's 1962 *New Yorker* profile of Narayan seems, in retrospect, to offer a sad, ironic commentary on Blair's relationship with his most notable writer. Mehta, who noted his countryman's "innocence and elusiveness," described at one point in the profile Narayan's childlike enumeration of his best American friends. "There were John and Jane Gunther, who, he said, liked his novels; Greta Garbo, who took him to be a specimen of the Mystic East." In the midst of this recital he mentioned "Lyle Blair of the Michigan State University Press, who first published him in America and didn't want Narayan to be 'commercialized.'" [4]

Chapter 4

OUT OF FASHION

The 1966 *Ramparts* article exposing—and sensationalizing—Michigan State University's involvement in Vietnam effectively eliminated the Press's secret government subsidies. President John Hannah's resignation in 1969 was another blow that isolated Lyle Blair from administrators whose support was vital. Hannah had over the years been offered several government posts; President Truman wanted him to direct the Tennessee Valley Authority; President Eisenhower urged him to join his cabinet as secretary of defense.

Hannah had always declined these invitations to long-term public service. He might take a leave of absence, as he did in 1953 to serve as assistant secretary of defense, but he always returned to MSU. His strength was in his permanence, his continuing commitment to the school he had led since 1941. In the late 1960s, however, the campus became decidedly unfriendly to John Hannah or anyone who seemed to represent authority of any kind. Students protested the war in Vietnam, racism, dormitory regulations, and required courses in University College.

Years later, Russel Nye would recall the ugly student rage. Nye had an immense admiration for John Hannah. Early on they had quarreled over Hannah's shutting down the student newspaper. Together in 1953 they had defended faculty members whose loyalty had been questioned by right-wing zealots; Nye had dedicated a book to Hannah, and on numerous occasions written speeches for him. Nye was with Hannah when he delivered a commencement address in 1969. "The students," Nye remembered, "spit on us."[1]

In the context of these ugly times public service in Washington must have appeared increasingly attractive. When President Nixon asked him to serve as director of the Agency for International Development, Hannah accepted.

THE FATES TURN UNKIND

After Hannah's resignation, Walter Adams, a liberal economics professor, was appointed acting president. Hannah's heir-apparent, Howard "Jake" Neville, an administrator Blair viewed with "unqualified enthusiasm," soon resigned and accepted a position as president of Claremont Men's College in California. After these departures, Lyle Blair would never again have the full confidence and support of a Michigan State University administration.

Blair and Walter Adams had at one time been friends. Adams had served on the Press's Board of Directors and Blair had published two books that Adams coauthored with John Garrity, *The World is Our Campus* in 1960 and *From Main Street to the Left Bank: Students and Scholars Abroad* in 1959. Adams credited Blair's "sensitive guidance and sage advice" with "whatever recognition this book is likely to attain." It attained a great deal of recognition, an editorial in the *Wall Street Journal*, and generous reviews.

For a variety of reasons their friendship did not survive Adams's elevation to the Michigan State University presidency in 1969. This might well have been another example of a Henry Adams aphorism coined when his old friend John Hay became secretary of state in 1898: "A friend in power is a friend lost."

Walter Adams's own account of his brief experience in the president's office is described in lively detail in *The Test* (1971). This most readable history of Michigan State University never mentions Blair or MSU Press, but it does present a system of values, a vision of a university that Blair would have found disagreeable. For one thing, Adams's dim view of "professor mercenaries" working in CIA-funded programs would have appeared to Blair as ignorant isolationism. Adams's willingness to share power with students and his conviction that student service on committees might be educational and de-radicalizing would also have outraged Blair. When Adams appointed students to the Press's Board of Directors Blair was furious. In his correspondence, Blair denounced Adams as a "thug," who had enriched himself through Washington connections. As late as 1985, the former press director raged against Adams for putting students on the Press's board. "The less said about him," Blair concluded, "the better."

Blair, seeing his press at risk, began some long-distance manipulations. On 5 November 1969 he wrote John Hannah, suggesting that the former president, now in Washington, arrange a meeting between former provost Neville and future president Clifton Wharton Jr.

Paul Varg and I were having lunch the other day and, naturally enough, were discussing the state of the University. The new President's visits have been carefully manipulated by Adams with Dr. Wharton being introduced to those people Adams wishes him to meet—at any rate for any length of time. Paul said it was a pity that Wharton and Jake could not meet for a couple of days. I have been thinking over this remark and I thought that if you knew Wharton well enough you might like to suggest to him that he slipped out to Claremont and pay a call of Jake and got the benefit of his views. I think such a meeting would be invaluable to him.

There is no evidence that Wharton ever "slipped out" to California to consult with the former provost, but on 11 November Blair did report to Neville his efforts to influence Wharton through Hannah.

I had it on the grapevine that Wharton and Mrs. Wharton dined with Uncle John and Mrs. Hannah at the Cosmos Club in Washington last Friday evening. Whether my letter would have reached him by then is doubtful but I am hoping for the best.

Clifton Wharton and Walter Adams

Blair's grapevine was remarkably accurate. On 12 November John Hannah wrote a "Dear Cliff" letter to Wharton, who remained at his New York post with the Agricultural Development Council. After expressing his pleasure in seeing the Whartons, Hannah noted that he was forwarding two letters. The first, from Jack Breslin, indicated his desire for a private and confidential conversation with the newly appointed MSU president. The second was Lyle Blair's 5 November letter recommending a Wharton-Neville visit. In forwarding Blair's correspondence, Hannah included this enthusiastic endorsement:

> Lyle Blair is an interesting fellow. He is an Australian that built the MSU Press from nothing to one of the outstanding university presses in America. What is more noteworthy is that he made it pay its own way every step of the road. He is exceedingly competent. You will never have known anyone quite like him but you can count on him to get his job done well. He came to East Lansing with all the usual prejudices of a British educated person and has become one of the best salesmen in the world for land grant education. The suggestion that he makes coming from Paul Varg as well as Lyle Blair is a good one, and I regret that I wasn't smart enough to make it myself.

Ironically, Hannah's note to Clifton Wharton praised Blair for doing what he could no longer do—make the Press pay for itself. Even before Hannah's departure, it had begun a headlong tumble toward insolvency. The Press needed a reliable, predictable university subsidy. As Blair explained to Provost Howard Neville in a 14 April 1969 memo, "It should be emphasized that the only support we get from the university is the sum of $14,000 and office space. This compares with the support of $130,000 accorded to the University of Florida Press, approximately $160,000 accorded to the University of Southern Illinois Press and approximately $180,000 accorded to Indiana University Press."

THE PRESS IGNORED

Blair's ability to make the Press "pay its own way" was an extraordinarily complex matter involving secret government subsidies. Financing had always been uncertain, a matter of improvisation rather than predictable institutionalized policy. In the early days, when the Press flourished, Blair loved to boast of his independence and his ability to run a first-rate press on a fifth-rate subsidy. In 1958 when he recruited Jack Gallagher as managing editor, Blair boasted of his financial independence. Gallagher, who wanted $10,000 a year, had been discouraged by a dean who thought that sum beyond the budget. "I think," Blair wrote Gallagher, "that you underestimate us a little, and that I could afford to pay you ten thousand a year even if the university could not."

In these years the Press also had a substantial income from the printing of Basic College materials. As the university enrollment grew, the Press's revenue from these instructional materials increased, although as we have seen in the battle over the "Comm. Skills" syllabus, this income was not unearned. In fact, the instructional services income served to conceal the structural, institutional flaws in the Press's financing. Funding during the best years was based on a fragile, uncertain political foundation. Locally, it rested on the Basic College (now cosmetically renamed University College), its huge required courses, and its rigidly enforced general education ideology. Nationally, the Press was at least partially dependent on anti-Communist ideology and cold war propaganda funds. Student protests against the war in Vietnam made the Press's cooperation with government agencies ill-advised if not impossible. In 1980 University College, which had been created in controversy and criticized and ridiculed over the years, finally fell and with it the Press's financial underpinning, the steady and predictable profits from syllabi and course materials.

Throughout the 1970s Blair struggled to preserve his press. The courtship of Clifton Wharton Jr., begun even before he was installed as president, now extended to Mrs. Wharton who had a keen interest in Asian art. Blair's 17 December 1970 Christmas greeting to the Whartons included some unique gifts—and an invitation to share in the pride of publishing:

> Under separate cover I am sending you a set of the books by R. K. Narayan published by us. Each book is a first edition and I think that you would like to have them in your library. Narayan is a strong candidate for the Nobel Prize in literature and I am particularly proud of the fact that this University introduced him to the United States.

Blair's attempts to interest Mrs. Wharton in scholarly publishing at Michigan State University were frustrating and ultimately futile. The Press never published Mrs. Wharton's book, *Contemporary Artists of Malaysia*, and the director of the Press never got close to the president. Blair's basic strategy, "educate them and keep them educated" about publishing, was far more difficult in a university whose size—and bureaucracy—had grown dramatically since 1952, when Blair had direct and frequent access to John Hannah. In the 1970s Professor Blair's crash course in publishing necessarily took the form of a correspondence course.

Blair was now required to report to the provost rather than to the president. This might have been sound "flowchart" wisdom, or it may have indicated that the aggressive press director had become a pest, or worse, that he and the Press were known to be contaminated by cooperation with secretive government agencies. Wharton, while working for the Rockefeller Foundation, had been stationed in Malaysia and had directed programs in Vietnam, Thailand, and Laos. His knowledge of Lyle Blair might not have been limited to John Hannah's "interesting fellow" letter.

In any event, Blair's access to the president's office was blocked and he was now dealing with minor bureaucrats. The various internal auditors must have been especially irritating. They demanded detailed financial reports, and one even bothered Blair about the "security" of the books in stock when the Press staff was having a coffee break.

In a July 1972 letter to Wharton, Blair sent a mixed message of good and bad news.

> In spite of a good year, we must not look to the future other than with gloom. Much of our improvement has been achieved by ruthless sacrifice but costs continue to soar. Salaries and staff benefits increase. Costs of paper, printing and binding will go up 6 percent—price freeze or no price freeze—on April 1, 1973. The Xerox machines hum merrily in the libraries of the country printing out materials without compensation and continue cutting into our most valuable market.

This same letter to President Wharton included a copy of a letter from Carroll Brown congratulating Blair and his managing editor Jean Busfield for "a stunning achievement." They were, Brown wrote, "running the most remarkable and successful small publishing house I have seen. I admire your achievement, your courage, and foresee even better when once again there is more with which to work."

In 1972 Blair decided to conduct the education of his (administrative) superiors in public. This was probably not a wise or prudent decision, but it did place the plight of the Press in both the student newspaper and the faculty newsletter. On 21 January, the *MSU News Bulletin* featured an interview with the Director who reflected on his twenty-one years at the Press. Blair explained the function of an academic press and plugged his latest publications, *Suffragists and Democrats: The Politics of Woman Suffrage in America* by David Morgan and *Broadcasting and Government* by Walter

Emery. Blair also used the occasion to publicize the administration's neglect of the Press. The Press, he explained, once had sixteen employees, but was now reduced to four—himself, associate editor Jean Busfield, and two office assistants. Blair mentioned the $14,400 annual subsidy and his attempt to control expenditures, including the recent resignation from the Association of American University Presses.

On 5 October 1972 Blair shared his concerns with readers of the student newspaper, the *State News*. Again he mentioned the modest $14,400 subsidy and lamented that current costs for producing thirteen manuscripts would be about $70,000. His staff had now been cut down to three full-time workers and three part-time students. The article featured a photograph of Blair. Grim and gloomy, Blair's face seemed to dramatize the pain and panic of a desperate man.

Blair's publicizing of the Press's financial problems did not inspire any spontaneous outbursts of support from either the students or the faculty. The students, who would protest almost anything in those days, were not yet sufficiently educated to see the value of a university press. Faculty members who would presumably have had a vital interest in the continuing existence of the university press, may have had their own reasons for failing to rally around the beleaguered press director. Some may even have viewed Blair's pain with a satisfying *schadenfreude*.

Blair had over the years published a number of MSU's faculty members' books; these were generally outstanding. He had never sacrificed quality for cronyism, however, and, given his style, one can assume that many rejected manuscripts left wounds and enemies. In addition to rejecting faculty members' manuscripts, Blair had helped formulate a university policy that prevented faculty members from profiting from requiring students to buy their own books.

In a 13 May 1964 letter to Provost Howard Neville, Blair recalled the old policy regulating faculty's use of their own books. The old policy required only discretion and left the implementation to Blair, "with the consequent unpopularity that comes from such an endeavor." Blair now felt that the growth in enrollment called for a new requirement that "faculty using his own books in class should feel obligated for the sake of both his students and the institution to see to it that he in no way profits from the situation and that he surrenders all royalties accrued from such sales to the scholarship fund of this university."

By 1974 Blair had managed to raise the Press subsidy to only $15,000 a year, but his optimism and curious pride led him, at least in public forums, to boast about the Press achievements in the midst of poverty.

The result in many cases was a mixed message of almost manic-depressive ambivalence. Depending on his audience, the sky was falling or the sky was the limit. A 1974 letter prepared for Gene Shallit's NBC television report on university presses offered a remarkably optimistic view.

> We are a small press. We publish between twelve and twenty books a year. This is partly because of the fact that the university can only support us to the tune of $16,000 a year. This means that we have to run an extremely tight ship and the staff consists of myself and two very able co-workers, Jean Busfield and Joyce Burrell. In addition, we have two student helpers, a part time copy editor and a part time production man whom we share with three other New York publishers.
>
> . . . In drawing up a yearly budget, it is my practice to predict a loss so the university knows what they will be faced with if the worst comes to the worst. But I am happy to say that in the 23 years I have been with the press, the worst has not yet happened.

When reporting on the condition of the Press, Blair seemed to be most candid with his peers, the other university press directors in the Association of American University Presses. His letters to his friends in this select group are more straightforward, without the ambivalence that so often undermined the message of his official internal communications. Consequently, Blair's relationship with—and subsequent resignation from—this professional group is of some significance.

On 12 November 1969 Blair shared his concerns with AAUP friends Mid Muntyan, director of the University of Illinois Press; Bernard Perry, director of Indiana University Press; and Vern Sternberg, director of the Southern Illinois University Press.

> We have a political board of trustees and they are pushing up clerical and classified salaries at the rate of ten to twelve percent per annum—to say nothing of fringe benefits. Nineteen year old clerks can earn nearly $16,000 a year. This is a situation we cannot control. Nor, since the university has been unionized, is it easy to get rid of incompetent help.

Although Blair had been a leader in the AAUP for years, he reluctantly decided in 1970 that membership in the association was just too expensive. The Press's Board of Trustees was "scandalized to hear that dues were $800," and "equally scandalized" that participation in the association cost another $1,000 each year. Russel Nye, a member of the Board of

Directors, remarked, "And I get $50.00 to attend MLA."

In another candid letter to John Irvin Jr., director of the University of Minnesota Press, Blair explained:

> We have a new president, a new Vice President for Finance, and a new Provost and I am not very confident that any one of them is particularly interested in the Press. Fashions change and I suspect we are out of fashion. I don't know what the future holds and all I can do at the moment is try to hold things together and hope for the best. Should we ever become prosperous again we will, of course, apply to rejoin the association. I would hate it thought that we withdrew in a fit of pique.

DESPERATE OPTIMISM

Once Michigan State University Press resigned from the Association of American University Presses rumors circulated that it had been shut down. When stories appeared in the *New York Times* Blair wrote demanding a correction and asserted that in spite of economies, "we are conducting a small but vigorous and profitable program."

Six years after setting the *New York Times* straight about Michigan State University's resignation from the AAUP, Blair learned that a *Publishers Weekly* survey of Midwestern publishing had also reported the death of the Press at MSU. Blair's response was prompt. "About two or three years ago the *New York Times* buried us prematurely and refused to publish a retraction. It seems to me your survey threw further dirt on the non-existent grave." In a postscript Blair added, "our income exceeded our expenditures by $30,000 for the year just ended. Not bad for a corpse."

Blair's feisty response to *Publishers Weekly* could not obscure the fact that the Press was in serious trouble; it was undeniably alive, but years of institutional neglect had left it in critical condition. The failure of the Press in these post-Hannah years was not Blair's failure, although he certainly contributed to it. His combative personality needlessly alienated faculty members and his personal relationship with John Hannah put the Press beyond the scrutiny—or interest—of other administrators.

The problems were not unique to Michigan State University. An academic press, a potentially profitable enterprise, is an anomaly in any nonprofit institution. If the Press is successful, it is ignored and taken for granted. If it fails, it becomes just another supplicant at budget-building time—and a more expendable supplicant than students' services, the athletic department, or the traditional academic departments. A central problem, then, was the administration's inability to perceive the Press as an academic department of the university. No university would congratulate itself for supplying the history or economics departments with office space or electricity and no university would expect other academic departments to be self-supporting.

Another fundamental failure—at Michigan State and elsewhere—was the inability to appreciate the Press as a highly visible, hugely influential unit of the university. The books published by the Press were, in a sense, ambassadors to the larger intellectual community beyond the campus. At a time when substantial sums were spent on lobbyists in Lansing and Washington, the Press was neglected. While much concern was focused on the university's various "constituencies"—students, faculty, sports fans, minorities, and unions—the central constituency of intellectuals was ignored.

There are no doubt demographic studies of those who read university press books, yet they remain a mysterious group. The usual academic clichés, "lifelong learning" and "continuing education," do not adequately describe these people. As readers they are concerned with more than updating their skills or cultivating a hobby. They are students who remain students, students whose education gave them something beyond credentials and skills—enduring interests, scholarly values, intellectual curiosity, and, above all, intellectual needs.

Sports analogies always trivialize serious human activity, but the Press in its potential most resembles the athletic department. Both departments can generate revenue, publicity, and goodwill and both can entangle the university in controversy and corruption. There is no Rose Bowl for books, but there are winners and losers, and the winners are highly visible to readers of book reviews in newspapers, magazines, and scholarly journals. The readers of these reviews are not just fans; they are, more often than not, players—writers, professors, foundation executives, people whose decisions often have a direct impact on universities.

The decline of the Press must have been deeply disturbing to Blair, all the more so because it coincided with his own decline in health. By 1973 he had suffered heart attacks, tuberculosis, and a stroke. More and more his ailments kept him confined to East Lansing, struggling with economic and bureaucratic forces beyond his control. In a 6 February 1973 letter to author and long-time friend Allen Whiting, Blair lamented the loss of excitement in both his life and his publishing. "Since John Hannah retired a lot of vitality has gone out of the institution. In fact, I observed to one of the innumerable Vice Presidents that it resembled a Soviet palace of culture run by illiterate commissars."

Blair's best years were clearly behind him. New people were in power, new priorities were being set, and the Press, as he recalled, had gotten "lost in the cowardice of the moment." Blair struggled for a while, selling off reprint rights, the "life blood of the press," to paperback publishers, chasing subsidies for every book, even drifting in the direction of vanity publishing. Finally, on 1 January 1980, after a quarter century, Lyle Blair resigned as director of Michigan State University Press.

Chapter 5

A HOLDING OPERATION

When Lyle Blair resigned in 1980 he was succeeded by Jean Busfield, one of several talented assistants he had recruited to the Press. Several had moved on to more lucrative and secure careers in commercial publishing. Jack Gallagher, who once described Blair as "the best university press director in America," went on to St. Martin's Press, where Blair served on the Board of Directors.

Jean Busfield joined the Press in 1958 as an assistant to the director. She served as an editor from 1959 to 1965 when she was named managing editor. She had been Associate Director of the Press since 1966. These were the years when the Press published outstanding books that earned reviews in distinguished national journals, and Busfield had been directly involved with many of these titles. She helped to edit Clark Brody's *In the Service of the Farmer, My Life in the Michigan Farm Bureau* (1959) and Jan Cohn's *A Palace or a Poorhouse: The American House as Cultural Symbol* (1979) and John Hannah's *Memoir* (1980). Russel Nye, incidentally, played a part in the publication of all three books—he recommended the Cohn book to Busfield, edited the Hannah memoir, and reviewed the Brody biography.

Busfield had been with the Press during its most exciting and successful years. She stayed on into the increasingly bitter end because she felt something more than loyalty and admiration for Lyle Blair. They married in 1985, and she continued to serve an underfunded, almost moribund press. So it limped into the 1980s, an aging mom-and-pop enterprise, "a holding operation."

Busfield had served as assistant director for so long that when she became director in 1980, it was difficult for people to perceive her in that position, especially when Lyle Blair remained in the largest office and served on—and no doubt dominated—the Board of Directors. Busfield, moreover, might have been limited by what is now called "the paper ceiling." She lacked the formal credentials: a Ph.D., faculty status, and publications, which would increasingly be required of press directors. (When she retired in 1986 an unseemly—and ungenerous—squabble erupted

John Hannah's *A Memoir* **(1980)**

over her request for a one-year consultantship prior to leaving the university, a standard faculty benefit.)

As Press Director, Jean Busfield tried a variety of innovations. She negotiated an agreement with Wayne State University Press by which they would produce the Michigan State University Press's new titles. She also tried to start an alumni book club by offering a 25 percent discount to MSU graduates. Nothing came of this proposal, which may have been lost in discouraging assumptions about the limited interests and specialized loyalties of the university's graduates.

The Press in these mean years had to draw on its assets, sell off paperback rights for ready cash, and cannibalize its backlist just to stay afloat. It was on the edge of bankruptcy, a process that Hemingway once explained took place in two ways, "first gradually and then suddenly."[1] The Press, in fact, seemed to regress to its humble origins in the bookstore-printshop days of 1947. Handbooks, lab manuals, study guides, and texts dominated the publications list in these bleak days.

In spite of the impossible financial condition during Busfield's tenure, several outstanding books were published during the desperate "holding operation."[2] Rollin Baker's *Michigan Mammals* (1983) built upon—and extended—earlier scholarship. William Henry Burt, a Michigan State University professor of zoology, had published a book on Michigan mammals in 1946. New remote sensing devices now enabled Baker to gather new information for a monumental, authoritative, 638-page volume. The Press also published Lawrence N. Redd's *Rock is Rhythm and Blues* (1974), a work that measured unacknowledged African American contributions to rock and roll. Clarence Underwood's *The Student Athlete: Eligibility and Academic Equality* (1984) was a timely and prescient analysis of university athletic department management problems and a call for greater institutional accountability. Both titles earned respectable reviews and *The Student Athlete* was adopted for use in courses at a number of schools in the United States. Unfortunately Underwood's call for institutional accountability went unheard on a campus where accountability for the Press and other programs was highly selective and sporadic. The book failed, obviously, to generate an appropriate level of concern.

During her final years at the Press funds simply were not available, and Jean Busfield had to tell prospective author Professor Louis Filler what she told Syracuse University professor William Wasserstrom: "Our financial state is so critical at the moment (and the university can offer no hope for the next eighteen months) that we cannot accept any further manuscripts." This was a time when Michigan State University was, to use John Cantlon's oxymoron "positively poor." Only a few books had been published during those frustrating years. It must be remembered, however, that Busfield had been de facto director during Blair's extended travels around the world. She had participated in the joy of publishing during the Press's most successful years—and some of the zest and exuberance of those early years came from her. She is, then, entitled to a measure of credit for the best books, the books that helped make Michigan State University Press's reputation.

Lyle Blair's evaluations of Michigan State University Press's most notable books are not entirely reliable. For Blair, the best book was the latest book. R. K. Narayan's and Russel Nye's books turned up on every list, but Blair's choices for the best of the Press were often tailored to his audience. Thus in a letter to President Wharton, whose background was in agricultural economics, Blair praised Newt Winburn's *Dictionary of Agricultural and Allied Terminology* (1962), a book he derided in another context.

Jean Busfield

Sales and profits are likewise an unreliable standard. No one, Blair admitted on numerous occasions, could predict a book's commercial success. He was astonished that *Greenhouse Tomatoes* (1979) by S. H. Wittwer and S. Homa earned enthusiastic reviews in national magazines (*House and Garden*) and respectable profits. Another unexpected success, J. Murray Barber's *Of Tuning and Temperament* (1951) compelled Blair to confess: "When first we published *Tuning and Temperament* we had an edition of five hundred copies and thought this would last us a lifetime. We couldn't find anybody who understood the book and we certainly couldn't. However, since that time we have reprinted it five hundred by five hundred copies at least six times and sold the reprint rights."

The most objective standard for selecting the Michigan State University Press's most notable books might be the hopes and expectations of the founders. The Bookstore Committee members who had in 1947 petitioned President Hannah for a press had enumerated two definite advantages—more and better faculty writing and "prestige value." The Press certainly encouraged faculty writing. Arthur Sherbo, who edited several volumes of the Samuel Johnson papers for Yale University Press, published four books with Michigan State University Press. In 1963 he edited *New Essays by Arthur Murphy* and in the following years published *Studies in the Eighteenth Century Novel* (1970), *English Poetic Diction from Chaucer to Wordsworth* (1975), and *Christopher Smart: Scholar of the University* (1967). Other books by members of the Michigan State University English department included Adrian Jaffe's *The Process of Kafka's Trial* (1967) and E. Fred Carlisle's *The Uncertain Self: Whitman's Drama of Identity* (1973).

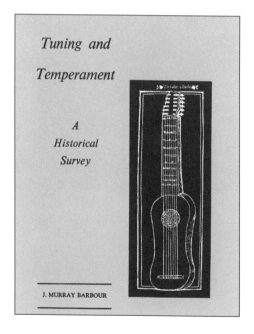

J. Murray Barbour's *Of Tuning and Temperament* **(1951)**

The history department's faculty also found encouragement from the university press. Paul Varg published four books at the Press. The first, *Foreign Policies of the Founding Fathers*, was published in 1963; his second, *The Making of a Myth: The United States and China 1897–1912*, was published in 1968 and dedicated to Lyle Blair, "who over the past several years alternately needled and encouraged the author." Blair's needling must have continued because Varg later published *The Closing of the Door: Sino-American Relations 1936–1946* (1973) and *United States Foreign Relations 1820–1860* (1979). Varg's final work included another graceful acknowledgment of Blair: "He represents a unique combination of the demanding editor, firm task master, and loyal friend."

University College professors, for all the squabbles over syllabi and examination copies, also turned to the Press when they had real books to publish. Thomas Greer published *What Roosevelt Thought: The Social and Political Ideas of Franklin D. Roosevelt* in 1958; Alec Gilpin published *The War of 1812 in the Old Northwest* also in 1958; Patrick Strauss published *Americans in Polynesia* in 1963; and T. B. Strandness published *Samuel Sewall: A Puritan Portrait* in 1968.

All of these works were significant contributions to scholarship and all, if they passed under Lyle Blair's "editorial eye," would be well written. Some, moreover, were reviewed in distinguished journals—the *Times Literary Supplement*, *New York Times*, *Wall Street Journal*, and *Yale Review*. Attention from distinguished reviewers in national and international journals certainly satisfied the hope of "prestige" articulated by the Press's founders in 1947.

Two authors, Lyall Powers and Herbert Weisinger, deserve more extended comment in any survey of the best of the Press. Their books were outstanding—and they inspired outstanding reviews from distinguished and discriminating reviewers. Lyall Power's *Henry James and the Naturalistic Movement* (1971) earned a splendid review from Leon Edel, author of the monumental five-volume biography of Henry James. Edel, writing in *Nineteenth Century Fiction*, praised Powers's ability to achieve what every critic attempts. His discussion of *The Tragic Muse*, Edel observed, "makes that cold discursive novel come to life." Powers's book, in Edel's judgment, was "a thoughtful, and one might say indispensable work on the Jamesean middle period. Moreover, it is felicitously written, always sympathetic, always 'critical,' and it is grounded in a deep feeling for literary value and the literary art."

Herbert Weisinger's classic study, *Tragedy and Paradox of the Fortunate Fall* (1953), has already been mentioned. *The Agony and the Triumph*

(1964), his collection of sixteen scholarly essays, most printed in scholarly journals or delivered before learned societies, must also be considered. The topics of these essays were diverse, their appeal to the general reader certainly limited. In short, this was exactly the kind of book that commercial publishers would shun. Yet this volume of essays inspired a review that says something about both Weisinger and scholarly publishing at its best. The reviewer, Laurence Perrine, was not uncritical of *The Agony and the Triumph*; for one thing, he expressed reservations about the title, which suggested "a Hollywood historical movie." After sniping at the melodramatic title, however, Perrine characterized the book as brilliant. "The author's interests," he wrote, "are broad, his reading is rich, his scholarship is thorough, his style is lucid and lively, the range of his knowledge is remarkable, and, best of all, though his speculation is daring, his judgment is restrained and sober, marked by sturdy common sense. He is able to look at his own intellectual predilections critically, and, unlike many scholars, he can mount a critical insight or enthusiasm without letting it gallop away with him. He is not at the mercy of the fashionable dogma, nor is he the advocate of the single truth or the one right method. He can neatly summarize contending critical methods or doctrines, and judge them with a cold eye."

Laurence Perrine's review of Weisinger's essays is a splendid example of the underrated art of book reviewing and eloquent testimony to the special service of a university press.

Several of the books published during the Blair-Busfield years constitute another special service, the ability of an academic press to reflect the unique strengths of a university. John Hannah's tenure as President Eisenhower's first chairman of the Civil Rights Commission (1958 to 1969) no doubt contributed to the MSU Press's early and, at the time, unfashionable interest in the Afro-American experience. The new edition of Thomas Wentworth Higginson's neglected classic *Army Life with a Black Regiment* (1960), Lee Steinmetz's anthology *The Poetry of the American Civil War* (1960), and Foster Rhea Dulles's *History of the Civil Rights Commission* (1968) would all have been of interest to John Hannah.

Continuity in Crisis

Another group of publications exemplify the continuity of commitment and the public service side of academic publishing. The Press's multivolume collection of President James A. Garfield's papers is a notable achievement. Frederick Williams edited Garfield's Civil War letters, *The*

Wild Life of the Army, in 1964. Three years later, Williams and another MSU professor, Harry J. Brown, coedited two additional Garfield volumes: *The Diary of James A. Garfield, 1848–1871* and volume 2, *The Diaries from 1872–1874.* Harry T. Williams, the Pulitzer Prize-winning biographer of Huey Long, reviewed these volumes for the *Journal of Southern History.* He characterized the set as "one of the most significant documents to appear in years," and concluded that the planned additional volumes "will be eagerly awaited by the historical community." Volumes 3 and 4 were published in 1981.

The monumental Schoolcraft project, begun in 1948, has spanned the life of the Press and required the energies of two scholars. Schoolcraft was a federal Indian agent located in Michigan's Sault Ste. Marie in the nineteenth century. His observations of Indian stories were an immensely valuable contribution to what is now known as anthropology and folklore. Mentor Williams, a University of Chicago professor, edited Schoolcraft's *Narrative Journal of Travels through the Northwestern Regions of the United States, Extending from Detroit through the Great Chain of American Lakes to the Sources of the Mississippi River in the Year 1820* in 1953. A second volume, *Indian Legends,* followed in 1956. After Mentor Williams's death, Philip Mason edited Schoolcraft's *Expedition to Lake Itasca: The Discovery of the Source of the Mississippi.* This journal, first published in a very limited edition in 1834, was reissued by the MSU Press in 1958. These works were reissued in the early 1990s and two more are projected for release in 1999 and 2000.

The multivolume Schoolcraft and Garfield editions demonstrate the Press's ability to undertake large, expensive, and unprofitable projects. Such publications would not interest a commercial publisher, and if not for the Michigan State University Press these valuable primary materials would have disappeared into the hands of private collectors or languished in obscure bookstores, inaccessible to scholars and effectively lost.

LOOKING BACK

In 1985 when they gathered with friends in the library to record their memories of twenty-eight years of academic publishing, Lyle Blair and Jean Busfield remembered their best books—the Schoolcraft project, the Narayan novels, and the Bramstead study of propaganda. The occasion was a bittersweet meeting with supporters of the Press, part postmortem meditations on the near death of the MSU Press and part celebration of Jean Busfield's retirement. They had lived through some discouraging

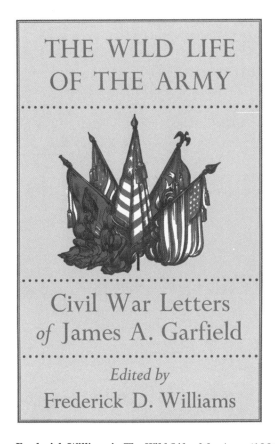

Frederick Williams's *The Wild Life of the Army* (1964)

years at the Press, but they had emerged with an unimpaired sense of humor. Blair joked about his hangover of 1952 when he learned that he had accepted a job as managing editor of the Press. His recent marriage to Jean Busfield inspired another good natured jest.

Finally, Blair expressed what might be the best epitaph for the end of an era: "Hannah left and I got sick . . . and there was nothing on paper to tell the story of the connection between the Press and the president."[3]

Chapter 6

TO REVITALIZE THE PRESS

Lyle Blair's regret that there was no documentary evidence of President Hannah's connection to the Press was not lost on one member of the audience who had gathered to hear Blair's valediction. Richard Chapin, the director of the Michigan State University Libraries, had a long association with the Press. Back in 1959 when Blair and Jack Gallagher were squabbling about Frank Harris's *My Life and Loves*, Chapin was trying to acquire the Harris papers for the libraries' Special Collections. Having come to Michigan State as a journalism professor, Chapin published *Mass Communication* (1957) with the Press and had served on its Board of Directors. Over the years he had become a respected and trusted insider.

Chapin was a major player at—or near—the highest levels of university administration. He had participated, innocently enough, in the Vietnam project. As a library consultant to the Michigan State University Advisory Group, he brought the Dewey decimal system to Saigon and organized the library of the National Training Center, a school for government officials. Over the years he had earned an enviable reputation for judgment and integrity.

When Jean Busfield announced her retirement plans the university asked Chapin to chair a Program Review Committee. The Press until that time had been adrift, unfunded, and apparently unnoticed by administrators who had more urgent issues to consider. This was a time when the university faced enormous economic challenges, as well as some attractive and expensive opportunities. The Wharton Center and the cyclotron laboratory, for example, were established in 1983.

In the fall of 1985, Joseph Dickinson, then vice president of the university, appointed a subcommittee of the Board of Directors to review the Press. The committee, in addition to its chair, Richard Chapin, included Martin Bukovac, professor of horticulture; Phillip Carter, professor of management; and Richard Dukelow, professor of psychology. Aside from Chapin, Linda Wagner, a professor of English, was the only member of the review committee to have published a book at the Press. Her loyalties,

Richard Chapin

however, might have been unpredictable. Her recently published book, *William Faulkner—Four Decades of Criticism,* (1973) had provoked a negative review by a former MSU student. Walter Brylowski, now a professor at Eastern Michigan University, had focused on errors that might well have been the result of sloppy editing. In a review for the 1973 issue of *Michigan Academician,* Brylowski noted that "the book is so badly proofread that by the time he has read the first essay the reader finds himself with a blue pencil in hand. . . ."[1]

The review committee was charged with the responsibility of analyzing the Press's relationship to the university, "and the functions performed on behalf of the university, the relationship with other university presses and marketing activities, and the corporate and financial status of the Press." Beneath this bland institutional language, the Program Review Committee was being asked to make a decision about the life or death of the MSU Press.

The Press was in great danger. Never before could it have been eliminated so painlessly. The fear of agonizing death throes that in 1943 had deterred Harvard's President Conant from "executing" his unprofitable press would have been relatively mild at Michigan State University in 1986. There were no continuing contracts with authors, no huge projects under way, no full-time employees to be eliminated. The director, Jean Busfield, was retiring; her predecessor, Lyle Blair, had been retired for five years. From a legal and ethical standpoint this would have been an ideal time to administer a gentle academic euthanasia to a neglected and seemingly unproductive press. Yet administrative officials hesitated, disturbed by vague dreams of prestige, haunted by nostalgia for a university tradition, or maybe just worried that the Press might, even in its moribund condition, have a constituency. The solution, of course, was to disperse responsibility by appointing a committee. The Program Review Committee, like all campus committees except for the Board of Trustees, was advisory; its advice could be taken or rejected and, if taken, responsibility for its decision would be dispersed.

By April the Project Review Committee had prepared a thorough, comprehensive, and evenhanded analysis of the MSU Press. They identified the Press's major objectives and considered the possibility of "alternative arrangements." Like the Bookstore Committee of 1947, the Program Review Committee identified the major value of a press as prestige, or, as it was now called, "image."

No one seems to dispute the statement that the image of a university in the academic world is enhanced by having an active, on-going university press. Most of the major universities, particularly those with which Michigan State University competes for faculty and research funds, support a university press. We are not sure that accrediting bodies, foundations, and donors ask universities if they have a university press; we do know, however, that when we ask the faculty if we should have a university press, the answer is usually yes. The reason for the positive reply is most often that of our scholarly image.

The Press's second objective, "To provide at reasonable cost instructional materials for use in courses," was now a secondary concern. The elimination of University College had diminished, if not eliminated, the need for this service.

A third objective, "to provide a publishing outlet for scholarly works," had to be shouldered by a large number of universities if books that were not likely to be commercially successful were to be published. Beyond this shared general service to civilization, the committee recognized that a university press could "assist the university by emphasizing academic strengths. A press can focus on such strengths by featuring publisher's series that will add to the stature of already strong departments."

In addition to identifying two major functions of a press and, in effect, eliminating a third, the review committee described six "environmental factors" that had to be considered in any decision regarding the Press. These positive factors, or "vital signs," indicated that the Press might be rehabilitated. For one thing, the Press did not have a cash flow problem. Although its average profit over the past five years had been a measly $1,300, the Press had not drained or diverted funds from the university. In fact, the committee noted that the subsidy of $15,000 a year was "not significant compared with the subsidies at other presses."

Another more disturbing "environmental factor" was the financial condition of the university. Faculty salaries, support services, and academic programs constituted $18 million of the year's budget. Funds for the understaffed Press would be scarce; even more uncertain was the place of the Press within the university's "mission statement." Some of the Press's original functions had been overtaken by technology or distributed to other units of the university. The committee noted, for example, that "the technology of book publishing" had changed dramatically. Computers and commercial copying centers were now doing the work of the Press. Other publication services were now offered by a new department under the Office of Public Relations. This office, headed by a vice president of the university, provided "little in the way of editorial review," but the quantity of publishing, "including instructional materials and scholarly monographs," satisfied "some of the objectives of a university press."

The review committee's analysis was followed by a list of four alternatives. First, the university might continue the Press "at the same level of activity." Second, the Press could be bureaucratically folded into a unit of University Publications. Purdue University had reorganized its press in this fashion to achieve economies and avoid duplication of effort. Third, the Press could be discontinued. Some people, the committee acknowledged, felt that "the Press had outlived its usefulness and scholarly publishing was no longer a major priority."

The fourth alternative, the one the review committee recommended, urged the university to accept "scholarly publishing as one of its top priorities and provide the necessary funding to revitalize the Press." If this decision was made, the committee insisted, the university would have to subsidize the Press with $100,000 per year for the next five years.

"A major university," the committee concluded, "deserves a major university press." Such a press should publish between fifteen and twenty-five titles a year and "attention should be paid to a regional responsibility for publishing scholarly works relating to Michigan and the Great Lakes area."

If the university would not make a commitment to support the Press, the committee recommended that "the Press be discontinued upon the retirement of the present director," and that the assets of the Press be transferred to the Michigan State Foundation.

On 4 June 1986 the Press's full Board of Directors met for a "special meeting" to consider the Chapin review committee's recommendations. The meeting was attended by several ex officio administration dignitaries— vice president Joseph Dickinson, vice president John Cantlon, treasurer Roger Wilkinson, and, of course, Richard Chapin. The board members, in addition to professors Bukovac, Wagner, Carter, and Dukelow, who served on the review committee, consisted of Erwin Bettinghaus, dean of communication arts; John R. Schwille, an assistant dean in the College of Education; David Scott, associate provost; and Gwen Andrew, dean of social sciences. The full Board of Directors discussed the review committee's report, and then, on a motion by Chapin seconded by Carter, they considered the recommendation "that the university accept scholarly publishing as one of its top priorities and provide up to $100,000 per year for a period of five years to revitalize the MSU Press."

The motion carried with two negative votes and two abstentions. The next motion, moved by Dr. Carter and seconded by Chapin, recommended "that if the first recommendation is not approved and implemented by the university, the Board of Directors of the Michigan State University dissolve the MSU Press and distribute its assets to the university." Dr. Carter's motion carried "unanimously."

The Board of Directors' first vote "to revitalize the Press" with $100,000 subsidy suggested some ambivalence. The unanimous vote on the Carter motion clearly indicated an unwillingness to continue with an impoverished and impaired press. The message to the administration was a blunt, unambiguous challenge: "fund it or fold it."

The review committee's less-than-resounding affirmation of the Press was not lost on one faculty member who had long been concerned with its inadequacies. Richard Niehoff, an assistant dean for international programs and a professor of education, wrote the dean of international programs, Ralph Smuckler, concerning his misgivings about the program review report. For one thing, the positive value of a university press could only be identified as "image." Niehoff noted that, "No substantive suggestions were made as to areas of MSU excellence which could be increased by scholarly publications of the faculty." The Press, in Niehoff's view, was dominated by the director's interests, which focused primarily on literature and the humanities. Professor Niehoff went on to list a variety of disciplines that were not represented on the Press's list of publications—physics, soil science, chemistry, biochemistry, biotechnology, and international programs. Their own book, Niehoff reminded Dean Smuckler, had been rejected by the Press but later accepted by Cornell University Press.

In addition to the vagueness of the review committee's report, Niehoff felt that the report was insufficiently comparative; the comments on other university presses were "minimal," with only brief references to Purdue and Northwestern. Niehoff wondered about the experiences of other university presses and raised the question of shared information: "We share information with big ten universities on all kinds of subjects—salary scales, library holdings, etc.—why not information on the presses?" Niehoff was also dissatisfied by the suggested alternatives. There was no "specific indication of how $100,000 (per year for five years) would be spent," and he doubted if $100,000 a year (even though generous) may give us a first-class press."

Niehoff's analysis of the report was better than his proposed alternative—"University Publishing Associates." This group was, apparently, a vanity press operation that published books with a minimum of expense and, alas, editing. This Niehoff alternative was wisely rejected, but his caveat had identified some persistent, enduring problems of the Press at MSU and those elsewhere.

The lack of a unanimous vote may also have weakened the Chapin resolution and encouraged Provost Lee Winder to seek a compromise. In any event, in a 22 July memorandum to the Board of Directors Winder asserted that "we are not at a point where we can commit up to $100,000 per year to the Press. Consequently, I cannot accept your first recommendation. At the same time, scholarly publications should remain one of the objectives of this world-class institution."

During his tenure as provost, Lee Winder had made some tough, unpopular decisions. Just months before the Press crisis, he had eliminated University College, the large undergraduate teaching unit. University College, like the Press, had prospered with the support of President Hannah. University College, moreover, had a large, politicized constituency who were, for the most part, loyal to the college. Whatever the shortcomings of this "general education" faculty, it included some very highly skilled office politicians and organizers. When confronted with the elimination of the Press, Winder hesitated, backed away from another tough decision, and instead proposed an alternative. Winder's alternative, the compromise of 1986, was to ask Richard Chapin to serve as director of the Press on a "quarter-time basis." Chapin, Winder acknowledged, believed that the Press post would take more than three-quarters time. The details of Chapin's time-management problems were easily waved aside: "Whatever, the Press and the library, both part of the total information programs at the university, can find a way to share his time."

The Winder compromise effectively saved the Press. The $100,000 a year was denied, but the Press was given a director whose salary could be drawn from another unit's (the library's) budget. The provost's office would also commit "up to $25,000 to the MSU Press for the 1986-87 fiscal year. With this arrangement, Winder expected that Chapin "should be able to revitalize the Press and, at the same time, establish a plan that will assure scholarly publication well into the future."

The Winder compromise must have been welcomed by the Press board members who sought to preserve, protect, and "revitalize the Press." Other parts of Provost Winder's letter were, no doubt, disturbing. Chapin, Winder observed, had only a few years before retiring. The final solution of the Press problem might, then, be deferred until the board had to make a decision on whether to hire a full-time press director. Then the Press—and Chapin's performance—would be judged again.

Another disturbing development was Winder's decision, "in order to expedite the affairs of the Press," to rearrange the bureaucratic flow-charts. "I will," he wrote, "recommend that the administrative channel for the MSU Press be via the University Libraries. There is precedence for this in that the University Archives reports to the Office of the Provost through the Director of Libraries." The Press may have been saved in the first paragraph of Winder's letter, but in the concluding paragraph it appears to have been demoted.

Chapin's "fund it or fold it" ultimatum had been deftly evaded. In fact, the ultimatum came back to him as a challenge—"you run the Press for four years." Chapin might have been dismayed by the assumption that his administration of libraries, acquiring and lending books, might somehow have prepared him to publish them. A popular movie of the time, *Goodbye Columbus*, featured an idealistic librarian, played by Richard Benjamin, whose crass and unsophisticated new friends assume that he's "in the book business"; Richard Chapin was now in "the book business" and he had only four years to succeed or fail.

The compromise of 1986 was not, then, a resounding affirmation of the University Press; if anything, the Program Review Committee and the close vote by the Press's own Board of Directors exposed the divided and uncertain support. For all the Program Review Committee's research and analysis, there was no final solution to the perennial problem of a scholarly press in a land-grant institution. Nor could there be, for new demands on the university budget, new priorities, new constituencies, and even new disciplines would make the continued existence of a university press—any press on any campus—problematical.

The future of a university press is by no means certain. A university press is the only campus "unit" that is not insulated from volatile consumer trends and unpredictable free-market forces. In the 1970s students shunned majors in business and sought "relevant" and "meaningful" careers in teaching, the arts, and public service. Never, it might be said, did so many compete so hard for so little. Later generations of students would likewise flee the once-popular history and English departments to study economics, accounting, and marketing. These consumer shifts may have influenced university budgets, but they never really jeopardized the temporarily unfashionable academic departments. A university, everyone knew, simply had to have a history and an economics department—and these departments had to be grown with patient, steady support. A university press, like other departments, must be nurtured over time. It cannot be dismantled and then reassembled to suit the fashions of the time.

A university's budget expresses priorities and values, hopes and fears with far greater eloquence than commencement speakers, press releases, or mission statements. Numbers speak louder than words and a budget speaks with the irrefutable eloquence of the accountant. If university budgets could be read as books, their presses would be minor footnotes to huge volumes whose major themes are more futuristic and fashionable, more epic, and, alas, more politically correct. A budget, of course, is not as rational or coherent as a book, for it is the work of many authors whose motives have been influenced by unseen forces.

A university's financial support for its press will, unfortunately, always be sporadic, unpredictable, essentially maintenance funding. A university press, if Michigan State University's history is a reliable guide, will lurch from crisis to crisis without the steady, sustained effort required to build a profitable backlist of books, the best of all possible subsidies. No president or provost will want to terminate a university press, but they will not want to build it up either. Given the demands on university budgets it is unlikely that any administrator—anywhere, anytime—will want to pour money into a "world-class" press. Such a press might be in the best long-range interest of a university, but budgets—and resumes—are built in the short run.

The press's place in a university mission statement might also be precarious and, at best, parenthetical. Mission statements are cobbled together by committees with wary eyes on the university's pressure groups. A press's supporters are neither organized nor insistent; they might not even be visible. Dr. Johnson rejoiced to "concur with the common reader," but a university press serves the uncommon reader whose unique interests cannot be satisfied by commercial publishers who aim for a mass market. Higher education, ideally, creates a constituency of culture and the size of this uncommon alumni association is one measure of a school's success

Joseph Epstein, editor of *The American Scholar*, recently defended the arts as "democratic elitism." University presses, like the arts in general, are elitist in Epstein's specially qualified sense of the word. "Artists [and scholars might be inserted into Epstein's sentence] are rarely from the upper classes." Artists and their audience constitute an elitism of talents "based on discipline, the cultivation of curiosity and sensibility." Democratic elitism, in Epstein's words, is a pretty good synonym for education. Elitist values and pleasures combined with the conviction that all students can be educated to share the values and the joys is not incompatible with the spirit of a land-grant university. Epstein's elitism is one that Justin Morrill and John Hannah might share.[2]

In the final analysis, support for a university press might be a matter of faith; faith that universities have created readers with needs that cannot be satisfied by commercial publishers, faith that the sons and daughters of "the industrial classes" might be both educated and ennobled. Such a faith, "the substance of things hoped for, the evidence of things not seen," might be increasingly difficult to sustain. American education since the time when Lyle Blair raged against "chewing gum" days in the East Lansing schools has continued to decline. Higher education necessarily shares in the decline of standards. Remedial education, grade inflation, and institutionalized student power—all these developments might be regarded as "environmental factors" hostile to the idea of a university press. There is certainly no guarantee that professors and administrators who will one day sit in judgment of the Press will necessarily share the scholarly values that academic presses have traditionally served. If books have never been part of a person's life, then a university press can never be more than an abstraction, another unit on the flowchart, another item in the budget.

Chapter 7

CHAPIN'S CHALLENGE

W hen members of the Press's Board of Directors gathered for their annual meeting in 1987 they asked the new part-time director "to put together financial figures explaining the Press's future and what would be required to break even." In the meantime, Richard Chapin was told that "the Press will make publishing decisions concerning new manuscripts as if it were to continue after 1989."

The board's minutes, with the ominous "as if," indicate the still tentative nature of the University Press. The compromise of 1986 was really a decision deferred; it prolonged the life of the Press but left its future uncertain and its potential unrealized. Chapin's challenge was to save the Press in the four years before his retirement. This challenge was both financial and educational. He had to convince skeptical administrators that the Press had something to contribute. He had to make it pay and make it matter.

Richard Chapin brought a new set of strengths to the challenge of university publishing in the midst of institutional retrenchment. An affable Midwesterner, educated at Wabash College and the University of Illinois, Chapin had been a journalism professor and director of the MSU Libraries since 1959. He was an administrative professional who over the years had built a solid reputation for judgment and integrity. He could disagree without being disagreeable, for he knew instinctively that friends would remain friends long after the issues that divided them had vanished.

Chapin began with a quarter-time appointment as director of the Press while continuing to serve as director of the MSU Libraries. He had a lot to direct. The Press was understaffed, underutilized, and near collapse. Only three books had been published in the past three years and a five-year accumulation of manuscripts remained unreviewed.

As an editor, Chapin was kind, compassionate, and courteous. At his press all authors—and would-be authors—were treated with respect. Furthermore, all manuscripts, whether they arrived with enthusiastic

103

recommendation from President Emeritus Hannah or came uninvited over the transom, were taken seriously. Preposterous, amateurish bundles of mangled prose that would have had Lyle Blair howling with outrage brought kindly and sincere comments from Chapin. One writer whose breezy manuscript he rejected was advised not to number the paragraphs when submitting it to another press.

As chairman of the Program Review Committee Chapin had very shrewdly promoted the Press as public service. A university press had little to do with crop rotation or livestock, but Chapin was able to link the Press with MSU's agricultural extension service, an unassailable function of a land-grant university since 1914. His initial goal, then, was to demonstrate the relevance of the Press. He wanted to "pick up on the academic strengths of this university and say 'this is what MSU is all about.'" He hoped to produce "at least ten books a year and one-half or one-third of these should be by MSU faculty members."[1]

Once installed at the Press, Chapin acted decisively to terminate the arrangement with Wayne State University. Henceforth the MSU Press would promote and distribute its own books and these books, Chapin hoped, would be profitable or at least pay for their publication costs. He aggressively sought subsidies for his books in East Lansing rather than in Washington. He convinced the MSU Foundation to offer a Faculty Book Award to subsidize the publication of an outstanding book to be nominated by the Press's Board of Directors.

Chapin was financially creative. Publishing to him was a cooperative effort and he had no hesitation in rounding up financial support from interested parties. Two books are especially notable tributes to Chapin's talents as a promoter. C. K. Dewhurst and Y. R. Lockwood's *Michigan Folklife Reader* (1987) was a fascinating introduction to the discipline of folklore and an invitation to view Michigan from the perspective of the folklorists. Written in a popular style, the *Michigan Folklife Reader* was an attractive combination of the scholar's insights, the travel agent's enthusiasm, and Chamber of Commerce boosterism. The *Atlas of Breeding Birds of Michigan* (1990) is another example of the Chapin style. The book had three authors—Richard Brewer, Gail McPeek, and Raymond Adams Jr.— and a list of sponsors that included conservation clubs, paper companies, forest service agencies, and Audubon societies. The book cost $58,800 to publish but because of Chapin's ability to bring people together it could be sold for only $39.95.

Chapin knew how to get into other people's pockets and other people's budgets. (He was himself on another budget; his own salary came

C. K. Dewhurst and Y. R. Lockwood's *Michigan Folklife Reader* **(1987)**

from the library's funds.) He began a "Publisher's Series" in Canadian studies and then in African studies. The editors of these series would be responsible for acquiring, selecting, and editing books in their disciplines, and their salaries would, of course, be paid for by their own departments.

Chapin's Press, then, was innovative, experimental, and unapologetically in pursuit of profits. If his books could publicize the university's strengths and show a profit too, the Press might be preserved beyond his retirement. Above all, Chapin steered the Press into new, previously unexplored areas, away from Blair's preoccupation with literature, foreign affairs, and what might be called "Australian studies." The Chapin Press focused on foreign policy, public affairs, art, music, and history: regional, local, and, for the first time, oral.

Chapin's first publishing project reflected these diverse interests and highlighted a unique relationship between Michigan State University and the Julliard String Quartet. A videotape entitled "Among Friends: The

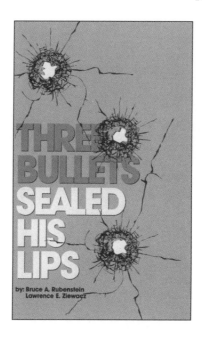

Bruce Rubenstein and Lawrence Ziewacz's *Three Bullets Sealed His Lips* **(1987).**

Julliard String Quartet at MSU" was produced by Bob Albers and mar-
keted along with a companion text by James Niblock, an emeritus professor of music. Funding for the video, which had an estimated cost of
$45,000, was made possible by a grant from the MSU Foundation.

Another early effort, *Three Bullets Sealed His Lips* (1987), brought the
Press into the true detective genre. Written by professors Lawrence
Ziewacz and Bruce Rubenstein, *Three Bullets* combined a historian's
research with the detective's zeal to solve a murder case, the 1945 assassi-
nation of State Senator Warren Hooper. The result was a popular and
profitable book that inspired an anonymous poetic tribute to Richard
Chapin:

> There once was a university with a hell of a mess
> Laughingly referred to as the University Press.
> To solve their great problem so very contrary,
> They called on the brain who ran their library.
>
> Quoth he in his well-known humble way
> "Finding me to run the show was your lucky day.

We will begin by shooting off the Bullets Three
You will publish and profit if you just stick with me.

The MSU Press did indeed publish and profit under the leadership of Richard Chapin. Philip Korth and Margaret Beegle's *I Remember Like Today: The Auto-Lite Strike of 1934* and William G. Ferris's *The Grain Traders* were both aimed at nonspecialized readers. Economics professor Louis Cain captured the spirit of both books when he recommended *The Grain Traders* to readers of the *Harvard Business History Review. The Grain Traders*, he wrote, "provides the human dimension so often missing in what many academics would consider more serious scholarship. This is not the meat and potatoes of serious business history. It is dessert."

MSU's traditional strengths in agriculture and international affairs were dramatized by Sylvan Wittwer's *Feeding a Billion*. Written with the help of three Chinese agriculturists, *Feeding a Billion* told the dramatic story of China's modernization of agriculture. This massive 492-page study earned a full-page review in *Time*.

Chapin's most notable book in terms of profits and publicity was Max DePree's *Leadership is an Art* (1987). DePree, the chief executive of Herman Miller, Inc. of Zeeland, Michigan, originally planned to publish his book privately, but "a gentle shove" from Peter Drucker brought the manuscript to the MSU Press. Drucker, in a shrewd judgment later used on a promotional blurb, wrote that DePree's short, 141-page volume "says more about leadership in clearer, more elegant and more convincing language than many of the much longer books that have been published."

The reviewers shared Drucker's enthusiasm. George Melloan, in his *Wall Street Journal* column, summarized DePree's philosophy of participatory capitalism and reviewed the extraordinary success of the company that manufactured the Charles Eames chair. John Greenwald, writing in *Time*, observed that while most management books advised corporate executives to behave like Attilla the Hun, Depree's philosophy more closely resembled "the gentle precepts of St. Francis of Assisi." DePree's book even earned a compliment from P. J. O'Roark. After a sarcastic survey of management books written by pompous and semiliterate charlatans, O'Roark praised *Leadership is an Art* for its uncommon brevity and decency. "Max DePree," O'Roark observed, "devotes his slim text to the idea of applying decency, charity, and common sense to business practice."

Readers, as well as reviewers, responded to DePree's *Leadership is an Art*. The hardcover edition soon sold out. The book was translated into

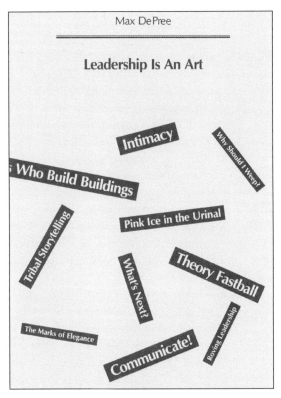

Max DePree's *Leadership is an Art* **(1987)**

French, German, Swedish, and Portuguese. The paperback rights were auctioned off to Dell for $137,000.

Another Chapin book, Carl S. Taylor's *Dangerous Society*, must have given a great deal of pleasure and pride to all concerned in its publication. This study of crime, drugs, and Detroit gangs might seem far removed from the scholarly classics that Russel Nye and Herbert Weisinger wrote for the MSU Press. There is, however an undeniable thread of tradition running through these books. Taylor's *Dangerous Society*, Nye's *Midwestern Progressive Politics*, and Weisinger's *The Agony and the Triumph* all represent a blending of the land grant spirit of service with the highest standards of scholarship. They all, to use Richard Chapin's phrase, reflect the university's academic strengths and say, "This is what MSU is all about."

The story of Carl Taylor's *Dangerous Society* is best told by former MSU president Clifton Wharton Jr. Wharton, in his foreword to Taylor's book,

Carl Taylor's *Dangerous Society* (1990)

describes the Presidential Fellows Program he started in 1970 to give a select group of students an opportunity to view university administration "from the inside." Taylor, Wharton recalled, came from a disadvantaged background that made him "an unlikely candidate for admission to MSU, much less as a fellow in the program." Yet Taylor flourished in the program, "soaked up everything to which he was exposed, and yet . . . never lost the ability to understand and communicate with his fellow students from similar disadvantaged backgrounds." Taylor went on to earn a Ph.D. from MSU's School of Police Administration. He became a businessman and for a time ran his own security firm. Eventually his assimilation of academic values and his sense of obligation to his origins led him to write *Dangerous Society.* "We are," President Wharton concluded, "the better for it."

Carl Taylor, it appears, wrote more than a book; thanks to Richard Chapin and the MSU Press he was able to write a bold new paragraph in the university's mission statement. Henceforth, a new vision of land grant service would include Detroit's urban youth as well as Michigan's rural farmers.

The decision to continue the Press beyond Richard Chapin's retirement was made without any melodramatic review committees. Chapin's books had earned profits, publicized the university, and said with compelling eloquence, "This is what we are," and "This is what we should be." By 1990 everyone seemed to perceive the Press as an indispensable institution. To dissolve the Press at this point would have been a repudiation of MSU's identity. The past had been reclaimed and Michigan State University was once again a place where books would matter.

Chapter 8

DOUBLETAKE: THE HISTORIAN
AS PUBLISHER

During his five-year tenure at Michigan State University Press, Richard Chapin fulfilled one of Max DePree's definitions of leadership. "Leaders," DePree wrote, "are also responsible for future leadership. They must identify, develop and nurture future leaders." In bringing native Michiganian Julie L. Loehr, assistant director of the Press, back from California and hiring a new director from the State of Washington, Fredric C. Bohm, Chapin assured a continuity of competence beyond his retirement. Loehr, after growing up in Michigan, had gone to California to study both British literature and computer science; her interests, no doubt, appealed to Chapin's own technological curiosity. He was, after all, the "futurist" who had computerized the MSU Libraries and acquired the Robert Vincent Voice Library.[1]

Chapin might also have seen something of himself in his successor. Like Chapin, Bohm had grown up in a small town, Bremerton, Washington, attended a church-affiliated school, Pacific Lutheran University, and then a larger state school, Washington State University in Pullman. It was at Washington State that Bohm received his Ph.D. in history and his experience in publishing; there he also helped to revive a moribund scholarly press that had not published a book in five years.

The two press directors also shared a commitment to land-grant values and a conviction that university press books could command national attention. Chapin's Press had done it with Carl Taylor's and Max DePree's titles. Bohm had done it at Washington State with works like William Hohri's *Repairing America*, which won an American Book Award in 1989, Clifford Trafzer's *Renegade Tribe: The Palouse Indians and the Invasion of the Inland Pacific Northwest*, and Sidney White's *Peoples of Washington: Perspectives on Cultural Diversity*, both of which received Washington Governor's Writers Awards. Small university presses, both men knew, could publish big-league books.

Following the recommendation of the Press Director search committee, Provost David Scott hired Fred Bohm as press director in 1990. This action signaled that the Press at Michigan State University would be granted a

Fredric C. Bohm

new lease on life. The university had the confidence to look off campus and out of state for a press director who was not steeped in the usual shared assumptions and comfortable loyalties. Bohm, for his part, brought unique strengths to the job: training as a naval officer, a Ph.D. in history, a book published at the University of California, Berkeley, seven years of university press publishing experience, and youth. He may have lacked Lyle Blair's contacts in the international literary and intelligence communities. He certainly lacked Richard Chapin's large network of local contacts, friendships nourished over a quarter of a century, but he possessed a unique "doubletake" of talents. He was both a historian *and* a publisher.

His family's origins were in Germany and Norway; they had come from Europe to settle in the Dakotas at the end of the nineteenth century. During the Great Depression his extended family became part of the vast internal migration that reshaped America in the twentieth century's third decade. Settling for a time in Bremerton, Washington, a gritty, shipbuilding town across Puget Sound from Seattle, his parents and relatives talked about the past. Like many other victims of the Depression Diaspora, they knew instinctively what William Faulkner meant when he said, "The past is not dead. It is not even past."

Conor Cruise O'Brien, the Irish historian, critic, and man of letters, has written about the historical inheritance that we all, to some extent, experience:

> A twilight zone of time, stretching back for a generation or two before we were born, which never quite belongs to the rest of history. Our elders have talked their memories into our memories until we come to possess some sense of a continuity, and the form it takes—national, religious, racial or social—depends on our own imagination and on the personality, opinions and garrulity of our elder relatives. Children of small and vocal communities are likely to possess it to a high degree, and if they are imaginative, have the power of incorporating into their own lives a significant span of time before their individual births.[2]

Growing up with enthusiastic oral historians gave Bohm the gift of history. His training at Pacific Lutheran and Washington State University reinforced the experience. Henceforth history would be a method, a mind-set, a way of being in the world. He learned to see facts in a chronological grid of dates and to perceive events through the shifting paradigms of historical explanations. Many scholars have this sense of history, but Bohm had something more—a sense of histories. He had an uncanny ability to envision unresearched, unwritten history and see it as it might one day appear in print. He could, that is, dream of books.

This ability to dream of books was combined with a curious seismological sensitivity that could detect faint historical vibrations from deep within unorganized archives. As he struggled to save the Press at Pullman, he must have sensed what Milan Kundera would later dramatize in *The Book of Laughter and Forgetting*: ". . . the struggle of man against power is the struggle of memory against forgetting." In dusty office files he found that Washington State University Press possessed a history. This rediscovered past gave significance, tradition, and some measure of protection to the present. WSU Press turned out to be older, more venerable, and therefore less vulnerable than was thought.

Early on, Bohm reissued in paperback one of its first titles. Originally published in 1942, Thomas LaFarge's *China's First Hundred* was the first study of America's original student foreign exchange program. This curious and important scholarly book would never be a best-seller, but as often happens in university publishing, the quality of a work's readers is as important as the quantity; *China's First Hundred* had at least one influential reader, John Hannah.

Press directors rarely get to meet the readers of their books or measure their influence, but shortly after arriving in East Lansing Fred Bohm had the eerie experience of finding a copy of the original 1942 edition of LaFarge's book in Archives, an East Lansing used bookstore. The work had been inscribed by Washington State College's president, Ernest O. Holland, and presented to Hannah five years *before* Michigan State College's young president would direct James Denison to establish a press.

The new director's vivid personal experience of that moment when MSU's history converged with that of WSU's dramatized what he already knew as a historian. The success of a university press is a cumulative, evolutionary, community achievement. John Hannah and James Denison, Lyle Blair and Jean Busfield, Clifton Wharton, Lee Winder, and Richard Chapin all had helped to build a tradition of scholarly publishing. Michigan State University Press, regardless of its legal status, had always been an institutional enterprise that said something about the strengths and weaknesses and, above all, about the mission of the nation's oldest land-grant institution.

While at Pullman, Bohm edited a splendid three-volume set of books commemorating Washington State University's centenary. The first title in the series, William L. Stimson's *Going to Washington State: A Century of Student Life*, offered a powerful combination of photographs and prose, ideas and images, that communicated what Irish poet Seamus Heany called "the utter, self-revealing double-take of feeling." In this volume the author and editor were able "to make hope and history rhyme."

Here, for example, is a doubletake from William Stimson's *Going to Washington State*, a photograph of four students from the class of 1926. The group includes a tall, skinny teenager named Egbert Murrow and the text tells the story of how a speech professor, Ida Lou Anderson, taught this boy how to be Edward R. Murrow.[3]

Young Murrow, in a letter to his fiancée, acknowledged the contributions of Professor Anderson.

> She taught me to love good books, good music, gave me the only sense of values I have. I've talked over in letters every decision. She knows me better than any person in the world. The part of me that is decent, wants to do something, be something, is the part she created. She taught me to speak. She taught me one must have more than a good bluff to really live.[4]

Given his historical sense, it is not surprising that Bohm continued Press traditions developed in the early Denison-Blair era. The tradition of excellence in Medieval-Renaissance English literature begun by Arnold Williams and Herbert Weisinger had continued over the years. This tradition may not have been the result of any single, conscious decision to develop such a specialty, but simply the enduring influences of old scholars' reputations. In any event, the tradition continues into the edge of the new century with the establishment of a special imprint called Colleagues Books. It happened when Colleagues Press, which was founded by scholars Robert Uphaus and John Alford in the 1970s, merged with the MSU Press in 1996. Current titles appearing under this imprint include *The Fayre Formez of the Pearl Poet* (1996); *The Wonderful Art of the Eye* by Benvenutus Grassus, and *A Concordance to the French Poetry and Prose of John Gower* (1997).

Another Press tradition that went back to the earliest years was the anthology of critical essays. In 1951 William Rutter had published *William Faulkner: Two Decades of Criticism*, edited by Frederick J. Hoffman and Olga W. Vickery. The tradition continues into the 1990s with collections of critical essays on George Orwell, Ernest Hemingway, and Harriette Arnow.

In the 1990s the Press continued to publish authors discovered by previous press directors. The monumental scholarship on President James Garfield begun by Frederick Williams was extended by John Shaw who edited *Crete and James: Personal Letters of Lucretia and James Garfield* (1994). Philip Mason brought up to date the previously published Schoolcraft titles, *Indian Legends* (1991), *Narrative Journal of Travels* (1992), *Expedition to Lake Itasca* (1993), and *Ojibwa Lodge Stories* (1997). The Press expects to issue a fifth Schoolcraft volume, *Thirty Years among the Indians*, in 1999.

In 1995 Bruce A. Rubenstein and Lawrence E. Ziewacz published a follow-up to *Three Bullets Sealed His Lips*. This time they expanded the story beyond the sensational murder of Senator Hooper to include the banking scandal that lead to his demise in *Payoffs in the Cloakroom: The Greening of the Michigan Legislature, 1938–1946*.

Carl Taylor's second book, *Girl, Gangs, Women, and Drugs*, once again dealt with the explosive topics of race, crime, and drugs in America's

Carl Taylor, author of *Dangerous Society* **(1990), and** *Girls, Gangs, Women and Drugs*
(1993)

inner cities. Robert Merton, the noted sociologist, hailed the new study as
welcome documentation of "the feminization of poverty." Marian Wright
Edelman, in her foreword, observed that "the crisis on the inner city does
not discriminate between genders. By taking us into the lives of a number
of girls and women who are confronted with the same hopelessness and
lack of options as their male counterparts, Taylor shows us that the
American epidemic of guns, gangs, and drugs is not solely a male phe-
nomenon."

While he built on the Press's traditional strengths, the new press director's earlier efforts were directed toward repairing the past. Some parts of

the past were beyond repair—for example, the rights to R. K. Narayan's novels had been sold off to keep the Press going during the darkest days of institutional neglect—but other damage inflicted by lack of nerve or lack of money could be repaired. In 1993—after a twenty-three-year absence—the MSU Press rejoined the Association of American University Presses. Full membership in this association ended a period of isolation and uncertainty. The Press could once again learn from the activities of other publishers throughout North America and evaluate its progress in various areas against their achievements. Comparative budget evaluations of university programs—sports, libraries, fund-raising—had long been routine. The MSU Press, by rejoining the professional association, announced its willingness to submit to peer review, and to measure itself by a national standard.

All press directors, at MSU and elsewhere, have had to combine their intellectual judgments with entrepreneurial skills in order to organize investors in books or finance subventions. Subvention is a curious fig leaf of a word that covers a multitude of sins in the publishing world. The greatest sin, asking authors to contribute funds for their own books, was once widespread, demeaning to all concerned, and potentially corrupting.

Yet university presses, throughout their uncertain lives in America, have had to seek financial help off campus. James Denison was uncomfortable with the practice until he learned that Harvard often demanded subvention fees from its authors. Lyle Blair, as we have seen, turned to secret government agencies, and Richard Chapin found support in Michigan foundations.

Press directors, it appears, have to be resourceful, imaginative, and diplomatic. Like Wall Street promoters or Hollywood producers, they must be skilled in the art of the deal. Unlike these more flamboyant organizers, scholarly publishers also must have a high degree of professionalism, uncompromising character, and a set of scholarly standards that cannot be sold.

The character of the press director, his or her commitment to scholarly standards, is absolutely essential. In fact, expanding new technologies make old-fashioned character more important than ever. In the age of the computer, every professor can become a desktop press director. While such vanity publishing is often condoned, encouraged, and rewarded, it is essentially a scholarly steroid; it bulks up bibliographies and creates a corruption that should never be tolerated.

There is, moreover, a Gresham's Law in publishing as well as in economics: bad books drive out good books. Once a topic has been explored, however superficially, in book form it appears to be occupied territory, and trespassing is discouraged. Thus the books and journals produced by self-publishers defraud the taxpayers, demoralize real scholars, and discourage the search for new knowledge.

Bohm's character and professionalism enabled him to achieve another major repair. The Press originally had been organized as a separate, non-profit corporation. The rationale, as explained by university attorney Leland Carr in a 13 January 1971 letter to Provost John Cantlon, was entirely defensive. "During the period of the late '40's," Carr recalled, "the Press sustained operating losses and was subject to improper pressure from the faculty to publish manuscripts that were without merit." A separate corporation was thought necessary to provide "insulation." The Press's independence, Carr acknowledged, had never really been exercised, but he believed, nevertheless, that a separate corporate identity should be preserved.

Over the years "insulation" had come to mean isolation and marginalization. Members of the board appointed by President Hannah were primarily loyal to him. The number of future administrators and provosts on the press board suggested that a seat on that body may have been a desirable credential for promising, upward-bound administrators. At one time or another, Presidents Walter Adams and Clifford Hardin, Vice Presidents Milton Muelder and Roger Wilkinson, and Provosts John Cantlon and Lee Winder all served on the board.

From the press director's perspective, the separate corporate structure meant university control without university responsibility. Bohm felt that a quality editorial board and peer review would be the best insulation against faculty pressures. The Press simply would not publish books without merit. He believed, moreover, that an academic press should play a more central role in the university. A university press is, among other things, an influential, de facto national tenure committee. It should, therefore, avoid both domination by faculty and isolation from the community of scholars.

The restructuring of the Press eliminated the separate corporation and placed it securely within the university's administrative structure. The Board of Directors was replaced by an editorial advisory board consisting of MSU faculty with a demonstrated interest in scholarly publishing.

Restructuring the Press was but one example of Bohm's ability to set the stage for the Press's second act which is supposedly denied in American life. The development and acquisition of journals was a major renovation of Press tradition. On two occasions in the past the Press had

had a chance to develop a distinguished "world-class" journal. In 1948 Press director James Denison decided against Herbert Weisinger's proposal to start a quarterly modeled after T. S. Eliot's *Scrutiny*. In a 2 August 1948 letter written just before he left for a term at the Princeton Institute for Advanced Study, Weisinger had explained the two types of high-level intellectual journalism to Denison, the former newspaper reporter: "The critical review devoted mainly to literature and the arts," and the "regional review," which is concerned with wider problems, and is not particularly interested in establishing a consistent point of view. Weisinger wanted a journal the caliber of *Scrutiny*, the *Partisan Review* or *The American Scholar*, but he warned that "once established, such a publication reflects on the institution which backs it and we should not undertake such a task without being sure that we can keep such a publication going."

Denison, always worried about money, failed to act on Weisinger's exciting proposal. Four years later another English department faculty member's promising association with F. W. Bateson's *Essays in Criticism* was also sacrificed for financial reasons. The English department's poet-professor A. J. M. Smith served as American editor for *Essays in Criticism*, but in 1952 he informed Bateson that "the new managing editor Lyle Blair" had "decided that financial losses of distributing the publication in America made it necessary to terminate the relationship."

Some forty years after disassociating themselves from *Essays in Criticism*, the MSU Press re-entered the realm of journals publishing. In 1992, Bohm hired a young editor, Laura Luptowski, to oversee the development of a then non-existent scholarly periodicals program. Luptowski worked closely with S. Tamer Cavusgil and the staff of MSU's Center for International Business Education and Research to launch the highly successful *Journal of International Marketing* in 1993. The Press then added two reformulated African Studies Center journals, *Northeast African Studies* and *Rural and Urban African Studies*. In 1996, the Press in cooperation with the College of Arts and Letters and the History Department, was selected to publish the *Historian*, the official journal of Phi Alpha Theta, the national honor society for historians. One of the largest-circulation scholarly journals in its field, *The Historian* is edited by MSU professor Linda Cooke Johnson; it is to Phi Alpha Theta what *The American Scholar* is to Phi Beta Kappa.

The overwhelming success of the MSU Press's journals program has been marked by the recent sale of the *Journal of International Marketing* to the American Marketing Association and by the fact that two other journals will immediately take its place. Beginning in 1998 the Michigan State University Press will become the publisher of the twenty-two-year-old

Dr. Linda Cooke Johnson and MSU Provost Lou Anna Simon. Bringing the *Historian* **to the MSU Press added a new dimension to graduate training in history.**

mathematics journal, *Real Exchange Analysis,* which will be issued both in paper and full electronic form. The second journal coming to the Press in 1998 is a new venture titled *Rhetoric & Public Affairs,* published in partnership with the George Bush School for Presidential Studies at Texas A&M University.

Bringing notable journals to the Press has been more than a mere public relations triumph. These periodicals offer unique educational experiences to selected undergraduate and graduate students, providing assistantships and internships, as well as part-time employment to support their studies.

Students who come to the Press over the years will learn a lot about both publishing and scholarship. Their writing will be enlivened by a concern for readers—serious but not necessarily specialized readers. Above all, their imaginations will be liberated from the tyranny of unattainable ideals. For instance, graduate students who read only the superstars of scholarship—Allan Nevins, John Hope Franklin, and Russel Nye—are often intimidated as well as educated. Highly competent journeyman scholars who make solid but not major contributions to a given field can inspire, educate, and motivate. The compiler of a critical anthology, the editor of an unpublished manuscript, or the biographer of a neglected historical figure are all realistic role models for those who would practice the craft of scholarship. An apprenticeship at the Press can add a new dimension to graduate education and make a valuable contribution to the making of young scholars.

By 1992 Richard Chapin's successors from the far west were proving to be an effective team. Bohm's understated, almost reticent, personal style meshed with Julie Loehr's extroverted energies to expand and extend the Press through publishing partnerships, mergers, and friendly takeovers.

The new Michigan State University Press *Lotus Poetry Series* is a case in point. It had been over thirty years since the Press had published creative writers, such as novelists R. K. Narayan and A. J. M. Smith, the gifted Canadian poet. In 1992 Julie Loehr addressed an Oakland University conference for Detroit Women Writers. There she met Naomi Long Madgett, the nationally known poet-professor from Eastern Michigan University. For more than twenty years Professor Madgett had guided and nurtured her Lotus Press, providing an outlet for young, talented poets, especially, but not exclusively, African American. Lotus had become a flourishing enterprise with a solid reputation in the subculture of poetry. Its list of seventy-five titles included the works of Houston Baker, the prominent critic; Gayl Jones, the novelist-poet; and Dr. Madgett's own timely anthology *Adam of Ifé: Black Women in Praise of Black Men.*

Despite the fact that Lotus Press had grown under Madgett's dedicated leadership, her energies and financial resources had declined over the years. By 1992 she sought out a partnership with an established publisher; her chance conversation with Loehr allowed MSU Press to effect a "friendly takeover." Madgett continued her affiliation, staying on as editor of the reorganized *Lotus Poetry Series.* Notable titles in the new MSU Press series include Bruce Jacobs's *Speaking Through My Skin*, Beverly Head's *Walking North*, and Adam David Miller's *Forever Afternoon.*

However inappropriate to the discussion of poetry, the Lotus Press would have to be considered a promising growth stock of immense potential. The 1990s have seen an expanded presence and influence of minority and underrepresented groups in American intellectual life comparable to the Jewish renaissance that enriched our literature in the 1950s.[6] For example, outstanding black writers, eager to explore and share their experience, have made stunning achievements in autobiogra-

Lotus Poetry Series editor Naomi Long Madgett and MSU president Peter McPherson

phies, novels, and poetry. The work of Toni Morrison, Maya Angelou, John Edgar Wideman, and Scott Minerbrook represent a remarkable burst of creativity.

The presence of the Lotus poets on the MSU Press list both reflects and extends the heritage of John Hannah. Previously neglected and marginalized areas of the American experience were now permanent features of a major university press. The most powerful and intimate parts of many heretofore hidden experiences would now find their expression. These previously ignored or inaccessible poetic voices would now be included in

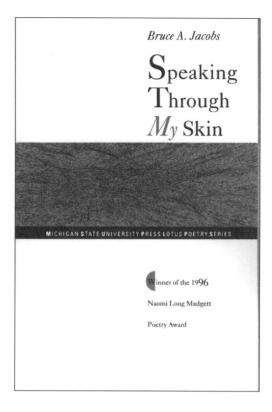

Bruce Jacobs's *Speaking Through My Skin* **(1997)**

Chapin's fine phrase, "This is what we are."

Attempts to repair the past, extend Press traditions, and assimilate new enterprises required the talents of a negotiator and diplomat, an organizer and a promoter. As a publisher, however, Bohm knew that his press would be judged in many ways: by the number of books published, the quality of books, even the physical appearance of the books. During Lyle Blair's administration, the Press had the services of artist and graphic designer Charles Pollack. His books, particularly his award-winning design for William Heist's *The World Christ Knew* and Russel Nye's edition of Richard Henry Dana's *Two Years Before the Mast* mark the beginning of the Press's interest in book design.

The tradition of the beautiful book seemed to fade away as financial support for the Press declined in the 1970s and early 1980s. Still, during his brief tenure, Richard Chapin was able to publish superbly designed books that give pleasure by the appearance as well as their content.

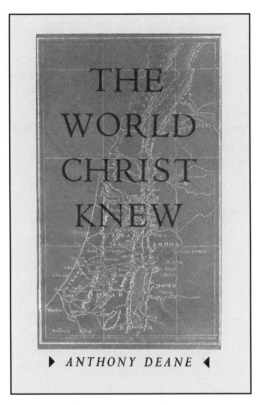

Anthony Deane's *The World Christ Knew* (1953), Charles Pollack cover design

Rewriting the Good Fight (1989) edited by Frieda Brown, Allan Compitello, Victor Howard, and Robert Martin may be one of the most visually exciting books ever published at the Press. Robert Motherwell's "Reconciliation Elegy" was an inspired choice for a cover design. Richard Brewer, Gail A. McPeek, and Raymond J. Adams's *The Atlas of Breeding Birds of Michigan,* which features dust jacket art by Catherine McClung, is among the most beautiful formal presentations of scientific data the Press has ever published.

Michael J. Brooks, a designer who came to the Press in 1991, firmly reestablished the Charles Pollack tradition of book design. Brooks's cover for *After Wounded Knee* demonstrates the sometimes subliminal power of a dust jacket. What first appears to be a striking abstract pattern of design turns out to be a photograph of a frozen human corpse. His jacket designs for books like *Essays on Modern Quebec Theater, Blacks and Reds,* and *Jacques Legardeur de Saint-Pierre: Officer, Gentleman, Entrepreneur* are integral

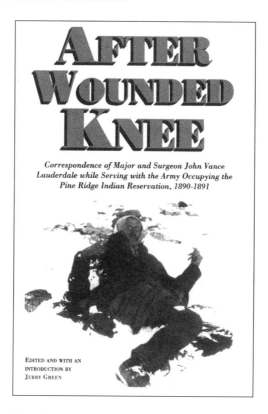

After Wounded Knee, **Jerry Green, editor (1996), a Michael Brooks design**

parts of the books. These covers have the appeal of frameable art and they serve, sometimes better than titles themselves, to communicate the themes of the book.

The post-1990 Michigan State University Press has not yet had time to define itself fully, but the outlines of a distinctive philosophy are already visible in the pattern of publications established in these early years. Although the Press has published books on film, painting, public policy, and business, its editors seem to have a special feel for neglected history—history made by ordinary, unselfconscious people who went to parties, made quilts, painted pictures, and wrote letters. Some recent Press titles—*Beaver Island House Party*, *African American Quiltmaking in Michigan*, and *The Ewing Family Civil War Letters*—reflect this quotidian history, which often goes unnoticed in standard intellectual histories.

The lives of African Americans have also been neglected in American history. Francis Fitzgerald in her *America Revised* (1979, Little, Brown and

Co.) anticipated students' brief and baffling exposure to Afro-American history in the most prominent textbooks of the past. There were, she writes, people known as "the slaves—who had appeared magically in this country at some unspecified time and had disappeared with the end of the civil war."

Scott Minerbrook, the author of a splendid new autobiography, *Divided to the Vein: A Journey into Race and Family* (1996), describes the effect of this missing history. "In our social studies classes there were still no books about the achievements of African Americans. In fact, the social studies textbooks seemed to use words in a way that excluded Negroes entirely from the tide of history, except as African Bantus or pygmies, or in their ever-present guise as slaves. I could not identify with that at all. My home life had taught me otherwise. I wanted to read more about Negro history."

Some recent publications from the MSU Press help fill this gap. Two books in particular might be said to rise above scholarship and speak to the general reader. Richard Hill and Peter Hogg's *A Black Corps d'Elite* (1994) tells the remarkable story of black Sudanese troops conscripted into the French army and sent to fight in Mexico from 1863–67. *An Enchanting Darkness: The American Vision of Africa in the Twentieth Century* (1993) is another such book. Written by Dennis Hickey and Kenneth Wylie, *An Enchanting Darkness* surveys some recent American images of the African continent. These images, promoted by ersatz scholarship and popular culture, were previously unexamined ingredients of American racism.

Four other studies of African American history might be said to desegregate significant areas of the black experience. Erlene Stetson and Linda David's *Glorying in Tribulation: The Life Work of Sojourner Truth* (1994), a biography of Sojourner Truth, presents the former slave's life in the context of the feminist and anti-slavery movements. Harry Reed's *Platform for Change: The Foundations of the Northern Free Black Community, 1775-1865* (1994), traces the development of black institutions in three northern cities prior to the American Civil War. *Blacks and Reds: Race and Class in Conflict 1919–1990* (1995) tells the story of the Communist Party's attempt to recruit members from the black proletariat. Written by Earl Ofari Hutchinson, *Blacks and Reds* is a fascinating analysis of the conflict between Communist ideology and Afro-American interests. The interests, of course, won out over the ideology and hope triumphed over hate.

Double V: The Civil Rights Struggle of the Tuskeegee Airmen (1994) belongs on the shelf next to the titles mentioned above. This study, written by Lawrence P. Scott and William Womack Sr., is another lively narrative that

Lawrence P. Scott and William Womack Sr.'s *Double V* **(1994)**

dramatizes the conflict between interests and ideology. In this case black and white interests were imperfectly united in the war against a common enemy. Black aviators, including former Detroit mayor Coleman Young, had to fight domestic racism before they could contribute to the war against Germany.

All press directors seem to have their stars, one or two writers who seem to leap out from the list and achieve a recognition that is more than scholarly, or regional. James Denison and Lyle Blair had Russel Nye and R. K. Narayan. Richard Chapin had Carl Taylor and Max DePree. For the Bohm Press in its seven-year history, some of the stars of the show seem to be Harriette Arnow and Richard Selzer. A physician-writer in the tradition of William Carlos Williams, Selzer came to the Press by means of a conventional scholarly work edited by a most unconventional scholar, Peter Josyph.

Josyph is a New York writer, actor, film director, painter, and arts entre-

Richard Selzer

preneur. His *Wounded River: The Civil War Letters of John Vance Lauderdale, M.D.* (1993) contributed to the Press's string of Civil War studies—*Trials and Triumphs: The Women of the Civil War* (1994), *The Ewing Family Civil War Letters* (1994), and *The Poetry of the American Civil War* (1992). In 1994 Josyph put together another book, *What One Man Said to Another*, a record of his conversations with Richard Selzer.

It was through Josyph that Bohm became acquainted with Selzer, and their friendship put the Press in partnership with this nationally known writer. Thus far the Press has published paperback editions of Selzer's short stories *Imagine A Woman and Other Tales* (1996) and *Taking the World in for Repairs* (1994).

Bohm's interest in Arnow began in 1995 when the Press published Haeja Chung's *Harriette Simpson Arnow: Critical Essays on Her Work.* While requesting permission to reprint an essay from Mrs. Arnow's daughter and son, Bohm wrote as both a historian and a publisher. As a historian he disputed the view that Harriette Arnow was only a Southern or regional writer. "Her stories," he wrote, "reflect the plight of Americans caught in the internal migration by economic conditions set in motion by the 1920s, the Great Depression, and World War II." As a publisher he viewed Arnow's work "as touching upon larger literary themes . . . that reveal the nobility and dignity of the human condition."

It was in this context that he sought to reissue Harriette Simpson Arnow's novels, "to make them available to the broadest possible reading public," and in the process make MSU "a center for Harriette Arnow scholarship." In late 1997 MSU Press issued its new edition of Harriette Arnow's classic *Hunter's Horn.* Unlike a number of earlier releases, the Michigan State University version will have restored to it a chapter that was removed after the Book-of-the-Month Club bought rights to the work shortly after it was originally published.

In 1999, the Press plans to publish a second Harriette Arnow title, a heretofore unpublished historical fiction manuscript, "Between the Flowers." This marvelous novel, actually Mrs. Arnow's second, was completed in 1937 and submitted to her publisher at that time. The portrayal of women in the manuscript was too strong, she was told; it would have to be revised. But rather than rewrite the work in such a way as to compromise its integrity, Mrs. Arnow simply put it away and it was all but forgotten for more than half a century.

In 1995 the Press also initiated its new Rhetoric and Public Affairs series. Under senior editor Martin J. Medhurst of Texas A&M University, the series seeks manuscripts that have national significance, originality, and a broad, cross-disciplinary appeal. *Truman and the Hiroshima Cult* by Robert P. Newman, published in 1995 to coincide with the fiftieth anniversary of Truman's decision, is a notable product of this series. It offered both a reasoned examination of Truman's decision and an original analysis of the "cultists" who, over the years, brought a religious zeal to their historical revisionism.

J. Michael Hogan's *The Nuclear Freeze Campaign: Rhetoric and Foreign Policy in the Telepolitical Age* (1994) is another original study that examines, as the subtitle promises, the interplay between "rhetoric and foreign policy in the telepolitical age."

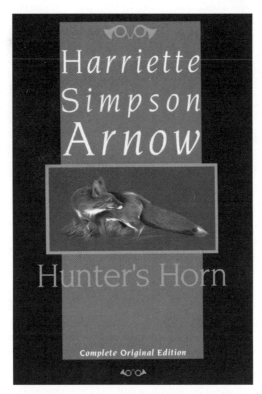

Harriette Arnow's *Hunter's Horn* (1997)

Gregory A. Olson's *Mansfield and Vietnam: A Study in Rhetorical Adaptation* (1995) and a title not in the Rhetoric series, Michael O'Brien's *Philip Hart: The Conscience of the Senate* (1995), shift the scrutiny of scholarship away from the overly researched presidency to examine leadership in the Senate. Over the next eight years, the MSU Press special interest in rhetoric and public affairs will result in the publication of a massive, ten-volume set titled *The Rhetorical History of the United States.*

The Native American series under the general editorship of Clifford E. Trafzer, professor of history and Native American studies at the University of California, Riverside, will publish studies in the literature and history of Native Americans by scholars of the American Indian experience. The first title in the series, Rebecca Kugel's *To be the Main Leaders of Our People: A History of Minnesota Ojibwe Politics, 1825-1898,* was published in the fall of 1997.

Other MSU Press policy studies offer solid scholarly responses to con-

Gunnar Broberg and Nils Roll-Hansen's *Eugenics and the Welfare State* **(1996)**

temporary events. Anne Greene's *The Catholic Church in Haiti* (1993) is a timely study of the traditionally conservative church's aggressive new "liberation theology," which cleared the way for more democratic rule of Father Aristide. *Quicksand: Israel, the Intifada, and the Rise of Political Evil* (1995), by Israeli professor Haim Gordon, analyzes the existential evil arising from the discipline of the social sciences and the policies of Israel.

Eugenics and the Welfare State (1996), edited by Gunnar Broberg and Nils Roll-Hansen is a remarkable examination of sterilization policies in four Scandinavian countries. Recently the work set off a firestorm of protest when a Swedish newspaper reported a portion of the work's controversial findings that, over the past several decades, as many as 60,000 Swedes had been sterilized against their will. Almost immediately, the Swedish government issued a formal apology and launched an investigation. Stories appeared in newspapers around the globe—editorials in *The New York Times*, *The Times* of London, *McLeans* Magazine in Canada, and *The Los Angeles Times*. Gunnar Broberg, one of the co-editors, was interviewed on the BBC; Ted Koppel's *Nightline* did a feature on Scandinavian eugenics.

All these books offer a unique public service; they were written and published with courage, integrity, and brave indifference to politically correct expectations. American presidents can order policy studies from the State Department, the National Security Council, or the various Washington think tanks, but the objectivity of such sound-bite scholarship is questionable. Truly disinterested scholarly analysis can come only from independent scholars, and their ability to respond to controversial issues requires an independent press and a mature university. At one time books written and edited off-campus might have seemed like "outsourcing" to faculty's trade labor union sensitivities. Books intended to provoke debate, disagreement, and controversy might have offended the fearful public relations mentality of some administrators. Such fears are perhaps the inevitable byproduct of the presence on campus of a press dedicated to the promulgation of new ideas. They can be allayed through the realization that responsible academic publishing, far from encroaching on departmental turf or injuring the school's reputation, enhances prestige and attracts new faculty. The recent track record of the Press shows that this is indeed possible. Clearly, the provincial fears of the past can be outgrown, and the MSU Press stands ready to help set the American intellectual agenda for the next century.

Chapter 9

FROM THIS SINGLE WINDOW

"**A**n institution," Emerson once observed, "is but the lengthened shadow of one man." This, then, has been a study of shadows, the story of how different press directors have shaped an institution within an institution, and through their books spoke to a world of readers beyond the campus. Throughout the past fifty years the voice of the Michigan State University Press was sometimes clear and audible, sometimes almost silent. In recent years the Press has reasserted itself and once again contributes to the American conversation about public policy and foreign affairs, history, and literature.

The view from the Press is considerably clearer and grander than the one I had as a professor peering over piles of student papers. Those who chop wood for twenty-nine years do not necessarily see the forest. Michigan State is a great university. It should not be judged by its weakest departments, its dullest professors, or its most immature students. From this window we can see beyond the petty rivalries, the office politics, and the corruptions of cronyism.

At Michigan State University Press the land-grant mission can be seen from a new angle. Teaching, research, and public service seem to blend into a unified life of the mind. Professors write not only for a few other professors who speak the same specialized language, but also for educated readers. Their manuscripts undergo a rigorous peer review, "blind" evaluations by anonymous scholars from other universities who are themselves unaware of the authors' identity. Here, professors have a chance to serve a larger public, to teach in a larger classroom.

At university presses we see professors working with students who, after experiencing the ultimate commencement, have become colleagues. Even after graduation the professors' work continues. They guide students' postdoctoral research, and use their contacts to help students get jobs, get grants, and finally get published. The best student-instructor evaluations appear in the acknowledgments of university press books.

This single window also permits a privileged view of administrators at work. Presidents and provosts usually labor behind closed doors and their personalities are often lost—or deliberately concealed—in the blizzard of memos and public relations pronouncements that sometimes seem to cover the campus. From the perspective of the Press, these same administrators can be seen making decisions, evaluating the merits of competing university units, negotiating, compromising, and improvising. Theirs is a high-wire act that also deserves some applause.

Whatever the fads of management theory, at the lowest level, assistant departmental chairpersons often present themselves as the ones who can best defend faculty members against the chairpersons, who are "real dogs." The dogs, in turn, argue that the dean is dangerous, irrational, predatory; and so it goes until we all believe that we must be protected against the angry lions in the legislature and, ultimately, the taxpayers. No such protection is needed. Michigan taxpayers have been remarkably generous in funding huge universities they might not fully understand. This history of the Press is, finally, a salute to all those who pay the taxes, write the tuition checks, and hope for the best. From this single window we can see the best.

ENDNOTES

PREFACE

1. P. F. Kluge, *Alma Mater: A College Homecoming* (Reading, Mass.: Addison Wesley Publishing, 1992), 8.
2. *The Michigan State College Press: Guidelines to its History and Objectives* (East Lansing: Michigan State College Press, 1950).

CHAPTER ONE

1. Gene R. Hawes, *To Advance Knowledge: A Handbook of American University Publishing* (New York: University Press Series, 1967), 29
2. Paul Parsons, *Getting Published: The Acquisition Process at University Presses* (Knoxville: University of Tennessee Press, 1989), 13.
3. David Murley, "Un-American Activities at Michigan State College: John Hannah and the Red Scare 1946–1954," interview with Walter Adams, August 1991.(Master's thesis, Michigan State University, 1992).
4. Max Hall, *Harvard University Press: A History* (Cambridge: Harvard University Press, 1986), 109.
5. Parsons, *Getting Published*, 13.
6. Hall, *Harvard University Press*, 109.
7. William Rutter and Russell McKee both continued their careers in publishing. After his work as a communications officer for the State Department in India, Rutter served as an editor for New American Library and the Franklin Publishing Company. Eventually he became Associate Director for Publications for the American Library Association. In 1970 he married Francis Ottemiller, the founder of Shoestring Press. They founded another publishing enterprise, Tompson and Rutter. William Rutter retired in 1980 and now lives in Vermont. Russell McKee became an editor for Michigan's Department of Natural Resources, where he edited *Michigan Natural Resources* and wrote two books; *Great Lakes Country* (1966), and *The Last West: A History of the Great Plains of North America* (1974).

CHAPTER TWO

1. Michael Howard, *Jonathan Cape, Publisher* (London: Cape, 1971), 33, 144.

135

2. Richard Chapin, interview by author, 5 October 1995.

3. MSC Press's publication of Narayan's fiction predated the University of Chicago Press's much-heralded first work of fiction, *A River Runs Through It*, by 23 years, Norman McLean's book was not published until 1976.

4. Robin White, "Fiction in India," *The Reporter*, 22 June 1957, 14.

5. Of course, not all of Blair's book ideas were successful. His curious scheme to have Russel Nye write a biography of Geronimo excited Marshall Best of the Viking Press, but Nye had other books under way and nothing came of the Geronimo book.

6. The MSU Press archives include Mrs. Baum's answers to unknown questions, presumably posed by Martin Gardner. Her memory of distant events was imperfect, for she mentioned Baum's opera house in Olean, PA. The conflict over *The Wizard of Oz and Who He Was* is discussed in my introduction to the MSU Press's 1994 edition of that work.

7. Maurice Hungiville, "Ford Madox Ford in America," *Journal of Modern Literature* 6, no. 2 (April 1977): 209–21.

CHAPTER THREE

1. Richard Gardiner Casey, "Australia: The Foreign Policy of a Small Power," *The Centennial Review* 3 (1959): 1.

2. Arthur Schlesinger Jr. "The Vital Center Reconsidered," *Encounter* 25 (September 1970): 89–93.

3. The CIA's use of intellectuals is discussed in Christopher Lasch's *The Agony of the American Left* (New York: A. A. Knopf, 1969), 63–114 and in Donald Harman Akenson's *Conor: A Biography of Conor Cruise O'Brien* (Ithaca, N.Y.: Cornell University Press, 1994). Blair's old friends D. W. (now Sir Denis) Brogan and James McCauley appear to have been open and principled anti-Communists. McCauley's Australian journal *Quadrant* was also financed by the CIA. Information about CIA cultural activities is still withheld. James Park Sloan, in his 1996 biography *Jerzy Kosinski* (New York: E. P. Dutton, 1996) notes that the CIA's involvement in books began in 1956 and was administered through the "book development" section of USIA, where "104 titles with messages supportive of the American point of view were published with either direct assistance to the author or purchase agreements to the publisher." Sloan reports that his FOI suit against the CIA was unsuccessful. As of 1996 the CIA continued to "stonewall," citing "national defense and foreign policy and protection of sources."

4. Ved Mehta, "Profiles," *New Yorker*, 18 September 1962: 51–90; Sloan, *Jerzy Kosinski*.

　　In 1978 R.K. Narayan was again "discovered" by the University of Chicago's Press director Morris Philipson. Edwin McDowell, in a 1981 *New York Times* article entitled "Publishing: Chicago's R. K. Narayan," told how Philipson, after reading a Graham Greene article about Narayan secured the paperback rights to *Swami and Friends*, Narayan's first novel. Philipson also acquired the rights to *The Dark Room*, which had never been published in the

United States. Narayan, now 91 years old, was featured in the 30 June 1997 issue of *The New Yorker.* John Updike's graceful tribute to Narayan does not mention Michigan State University Press

CHAPTER FOUR

1. *Lyle Blair Talks about the MSU Press.* Sound recording. MSU Voice Library, 1985.

CHAPTER FIVE

1. Ernest Hemingway, *The Sun Also Rises* (New York: Charles Scribners's Sons, 1926), 136.
2. For example, Russel Nye urged the Press to establish a relationship with Lewis Filler, "a brilliant scholar" who wanted to bring out a new edition of his classic *The Crusade Against Slavery.*
3. *Lyle Blair Talks about the MSU Press.* Sound recording. MSU Voice Library, 1985.

CHAPTER SIX

1. Walter Brylowski, *Michigan Academician* (1973): 251-2.
2. Joseph Epstein, "Why, Despite Everything, Republicans Should Not Abandon the Ants," *The Weekly Standard* (3 June 1996): 35.

CHAPTER EIGHT

1. Doug Collar, "Hello Prosperity: the Life and Times of G. Robert Vincent, Founder of the National Voice Library" (Ph.D. diss. Michigan State University, 1988).
2. Conor Cruise O'Brien, "The Parnellism of Sean O'Faolain," *Irish Writing* (July 1948): 59. As quoted in Donald Harman Akenson, *Conor: A Biography of Conor Cruise O'Brien* (Ithaca, N. Y.: Cornell University Press, 1994), 4.
3. Milan Kundera, *The Book of Laughter and Forgetting* (New York: Harper Perennial Edition, 1996), 4.
4. Seamus Heany, *The Cure at Troy* (New York: Noonday Press, 1991).
5. Washington State University acknowledged the contributions of their most famous graduate with the founding of the Edward R. Murrow School of Communication in 1970s. In the prosy world of academe Bohm's gifts go by the dreary name "interdisciplinary." Seamus Heany's phrase "double-take" is more accurate and more suggestive. In fact, it suggested the title of a wonderful new magazine edited by Robert Coles and published by Duke University's outstanding press. Heany's poem "The Cure at Troy" is featured on the first page of every *Doubletake* issue.
6. Francis Fitzgerald, *America Revised* (Boston: Little Brown and Company; Atlantic Monthly Press, 1979), 83.

7. Michael Berube, "Public Academy," *New Yorker*, 9 January 1995, 73–80; Robert S. Boynton, "The New Intellectuals," *Atlantic Monthly* 275, no. 3 (March 1995): 53–79.

Bibliography

The following individuals were interviewed in the course of researching this book. Some are quoted directly and acknowledged in the footnotes. All were helpful and gave generously of their time: Jim Alfredson, Eugene Balsley, Mitch Bloomfield, Fred Bohm, Richard Chapin, Maurice Crane, Robert Farrell Eck, Julie Loehr, Russell McKee, Russell Nye, Kay Nye, and Monte Nye.

Adams, Walter. *The Test.* New York: Macmillan, 1971.

Anderson, David L. *Trapped by Success: The Eisenhower Administration and Vietnam, 1953–1961.* New York: Columbia University Press, 1991.

Bailey, Herbert S. Jr. *The Art and Science of Book Publishing.* Austin: University of Texas Press, 1970.

Bogart, Leo. *Cold Words, Cold War: A New Look at USIA's Premises for Propaganda.* Washington, D.C.: American University Press, 1995.

Caute, David. *The Great Fear: The Anti-Communist Purge under Truman and Eisenhower.* New York: Simon and Schuster, 1978.

Collar, Doug. "'Hello Prosperity': The Life and Times of Robert Vincent, Founder of the National Voice Library." Phd. diss., Michigan State University, 1988.

Diamond, Sigmund. *Compromised Campus: The Collaboration of Universities with the Intelligence Community, 1945–1955.* New York: Oxford University Press, 1992.

Dorson, Richard M. *Bloodstoppers & Bearwalkers: Folk Traditions of the Upper Peninsula.* Cambridge, Mass.: Harvard University Press, 1952.

Dressel, Paul. *College to University: The Hannah Years.* East Lansing: Michigan State University, 1987.

Fitzgerald, Francis. *America Revised.* Boston: Little, Brown and Co., 1979.

Frugé, August. *The Metamorphosis of the University of California Press.* Berkeley: Associates of the University of California Press, 1986.

Fried, Richard. *Men Against McCarthy*. New York: Columbia University Press, 1976.

———. *A Skeptic Among Scholars: August Frugé on University Publishing*. Berkeley: University of California Press, 1993.

Gardner, David P. *The California Oath Controversy*. Berkeley and Los Angeles: University of California Press, 1967.

Goodfriend, Andrew. *The Twisted Image*. New York: St. Martin's Press, 1963.

Goodman, Walter. *The Committee: The Extraordinary Career of the House Committee on Un-American Activities*. New York: Farrar, Strauss, and Giroux, 1964.

Halberstam, David. *The Best and the Brightest*. New York: Random House, 1972.

Hall, Max. *Harvard University Press: A History*. Cambridge: Harvard University Press, 1986.

Harman, Eleanor, ed. *The University as Publisher*. Toronto: University of Toronto Press, 1961.

Hawes, Gene R. *To Advance Knowledge: A Handbook of University Press Publishing*. American University Press Services, 1967.

Heineman, Kenneth J. *Campus Wars: The Peace Movement at American State Universities in the Vietnam Era*. New York: New York University Press, 1993.

Horowitz, David. *Radical Son*. New York: Free Press, 1997.

Howard, Michael. *Jonathan Cape, Publisher*. London: Cape, 1971.

Kluge, P. F. *Alma Mater: A College Homecoming*. Reading, Mass.: Addison Wesley Publishing, 1993.

Kuhn, Madison. *Michigan State: The First Hundred Years*. East Lansing: Michigan State University Press, 1955.

Kluge, P. F. *Alma Mater: A College Homecoming*. New York: Addison-Wesley, 1993.

Madgett, Naomi Long. *A Milestone Sampler: 15th Anniversary Anthology*. Detroit: Lotus Press, 1988.

Murley, David. "Un-American Activities at Michigan State College: John Hannah and the Red Scare 1946–1954." Master's thesis, Michigan State University.

Navasky, Victor S. *Naming Names*. New York: Viking Press, 1980.

Parsons, Paul. Getting Published: *The Acquisition Process at University Presses*. Knoxville: University of Tennessee Press, 1989.

Rickover, Hyman. *American Education—A National Failure.* New York: Dutton, 1963.

Sanders, June. *Cold War on Campus: Academic Freedom and the University of Washington.* Seattle: University of Washington Press, 1979.

Schrecker, Ellen W. *No Ivory Tower: McCarthyism and the Universities.* New York: Oxford Press, 1986.

Schriffen, Andre, editor. *The Cold War and the University.* New York: The New Press, 1997.

Selcraig, James T. *The Red Scare in the Midwest 1945–1955. A State and Local Study.* University of Michigan, 1982.

Smith, Datus C. Jr., *A Guide to Book Publishing.* Rev. Ed. Seattle: University of Washington Press, 1989.

Stewart, George R. *The Year of the Oath: The Fight for Academic Freedom at the University of California.* Garden City, N. Y.: Doubleday and Co., 1950.

Weidner, Edward W. *Technical Assistance in Public Administration Overseas: The Case for Development Administration.* Chicago: Public Administration Service, 1964.

INDEX

Adam of Ifé, 121

Adams, Raymond, Jr., 104, 124

Adams, Walter, 72, *73,* 118

African American Quiltmaking in Michigan, 125

After Wounded Knee, 124, *125*

Agency for International Development, the (AID), 57

Agony and the Triumph, The, 88-89, 108

"Alas, Poor Peter," 39

Albers, Bob, 106

Alford, John, 115

Algren, Nelson, 27

Allen, George V., 34

alumni book club, 84

Americans in Polynesia, 88

"Among Friends," 105-6

Anderson, Ida Lou, 114-15

Andrew, Gwen, 97

Applegate, A. A., 13, 18

Army Life with a Black Regiment, 89

Arnow, Harriette, 127, 129

Ashes to Ashes, 28, 38

Association of American University Presses, the, 10

Atlas of Breeding Birds of Michigan, The, 104, 124

"Atrocity," 57

Auden, W. H., 29

Australian Encyclopedia, The, 33

Bachelor of Arts, The, 31

backlist, importance of to university presses, 1, 9, 16-17, 101

Baker's Dozen, A, 8

Baker, Rollin, 85

Ball, MacMayhon, 36

Barbour, J. Murray, 86

Barzun, Jacques, 29, 51

Beaver Island House Party, 125

Beegle, Margaret, 107

Best, Marshall, 68

Bettinghaus, Erwin, 97

"Between the Flowers," 129

Black Corps d'Elite, A, 126

Blacks and Reds, 124, 126

Blair, David, 48

Blair, Lyle, *25, 34*; as aggressive editor, 38-39; and American education, 39, 40, 41; and anthologies, 41; anti-Communist stance of, 27, 40, 67-68; and Austrian publishing house, 25; and the Board of Directors, 35-36; books written by, 28, 38, 39; and Clifton Wharton Jr., 72-74, 75, 76; and colonial/commonwealth litera-ture, 41; decline in health of, 80; and Emily Schossberger, 34-36, 42; and *Essays in Criticism,* 119; exotic background of, 23; faculty status of, 36, 52-53; and financing of Michigan State University Press, 26, 36, 74-75, 77-79; formality of, 42; high standards of, 26-27, 51, 52, 77; hiring of, 26, 91; and independence of the Michigan State University Press, 35-38; influence on Michigan State University Press, 27-28, 31;

and James Denison, 64-65; and Jean
Busfield, 83, 91; and "Looking for
Magsaysay," 68-70; and the Mimosa
editions, 64, 65-66; and *My Life and
Loves*, 29, 30, 93; notable books published during tenure of, 85-87; and
press director's faculty instructional
responsibilities, 35, 76; as professor,
52-53; relations with authors, 42-43;
relations with reviewers, 43, 44-45;
relations with university administration and faculty, 36, 72, 76, 77, 79;
resignation of, 81; and R. K.
Narayan, 31-33, 68-70; and St.
Martin's Press, 83; and secret government press subsidies, 57, 58, 65-
66, 68-69, 74, 117; southern cross
imprint of, 28; and *The Wizard of Oz
and Who He Was*, 45-50; and *This
Almost Chosen People*, 44-45; use of
past contacts, 23-24, 28; and
Vietnam, The First Five Years, 59-62;
and Walter Adams, 72
Bloodstoppers and Bearwalkers, 19
Bloomfield, Morton, 11, 21
Bode, Carl, 19
Bohm, Fredric C., *112*; background of,
111, 112-13; and Harriette Simpson
Arnow, 129; as historian and pub-
lisher, 112, 113, 129; and journals at
Michigan State University Press,
119; notable books during tenure
of, 115, 121-31; and reorganization
of Michigan State University Press
corporate structure, 118; at
Washington State University Press,
113-14
Bowen, Carroll, 53
Boy's State Convention, 12
Bramstead, Ernest, 38
Brattin, John, 13
Breit, Harvey, 33, 34, 48
Breslin, Lyle, 74
Brewer, Richard, 104, 124

Broadcasting and Government, 77
Broberg, Gunnar, 131
Brody, Clark, 83
Brogan, D. W., 39-40, 136n.3
Brooks, Michael J., 124
Brown, Benjamin H., 65
Brown, Frieda, 123
Brown, Harry J., 90
Brylowski, Walter, 94
Bukovac, Martin, 93, 97
Burt, William Henry, 85
Busfield, Jean, 76, 77, 83-85, *86*
Butler, Nicolas Murray, 1

Cambridge University Press, 1
Cantlon, John, 97, 118
Cape, Jonathan, 23
Carlisle, E. Fred, 87
Carr, Leland, 118
Carter, Philip, 93, 97
Casey, R. G., 57-58, 59
Catholic Church in Haiti, The, 130
Cavusgil, S. Tamer, 119
*Centennial History of Michigan State
University*, 38
Chapin, Richard, *94*; background of,
93, 103; book design during tenure
of, 123-24; as director of Michigan
State University Press, 99, 103-10;
editorial style of, 103-4; and *My Life
and Loves*, 30, 93; notable books
during tenure of, 107-8; and
Program Review Committee, 93;
and subsidization of books, 104-5,
117; and *Vietnam: The First Five Years*,
59; and the Vietnam project, 93
*Characterization of Pilate in the Townely
Plays, The*, 20
"cheap books" program, the, 65
"chewing gum days," 39
Chicago Renaissance, 8
China's First Hundred, 114
*Christopher Smart: Scholar of the
University*, 87

Chung, Haeja K., 129
Churchill, Sir Winston, 24
Clark, Harry Hayden, 19
Closing of the Door, The, 88
Cohn, Jan, 83
Colleagues Books, 115
Compitello, Allan, 123
Conant, James B., 2, 4, 95
Concordance to the French Poetry and Prose of John Gower, A, 115
Congress for Cultural Freedom, the, 67
Correlation of Some Physical Properties of Alkane and Alkenes, A, 6
Cousins, Norman, 34
Crete and James, 115
Crocker, Lester, 20
Cross Sectional Nomenclature of the Beef Carcass, The, 11

Dana, *Richard Henry*, 65
Dangerous Society, 108-10, *109*
Dark Room, The, 136n. 4
Darnell, Margery, 57
Dateless, Diary, The, 32, 68
David, Linda, 126
Davis, Richard Brion, 44
de Zouche, Mary, 23, 24, 59
Denison, James H., 7; as administrative assistant to John A. Hannah, 4-5; and financing of Michigan State University Press, 17-18, 117; and the founding of the Michigan State University Press, 5; and Lyle Blair, 26, 28; notable books published during tenure of, 19-21; and Russell McKee, 14; and the Vietnam project, 5, 57; and Weisinger journal, 119
Denny, Reul, 11
Denslow, W. W., 46
DePree Max, 107, 111
Dewhurst, C. K., 104
Diaries from 1872-1874, The, 90
Diary of James A. Garfield, 1848-1871, The, 90

Diary of James Strang, The, 8
Dickinson, Joseph, 93, 97
Dictionary of Agricultural and Allied Terminology, 85
Dorson, Richard, 18-19
Double V, 126-27, *127*
Douglas, Lord Alfred, 29
Douglas, Paul, 26
Drucker, Peter, 107
du Berrier, Hilaire, 61
Dukelow, Richard, 93, 97
Dulles, Foster, Rhea, 89
Dulles, John Foster, 60-61

East and West Must Meet, 65, *66*
Eaton, Clement, 8
Edel, Leon, 34, 88
Edelman, Marian Wright, 116
Eisenhower, Dwight D., 71
Elliot, William, 42
Embattled Philosopher, The, 20, *21*, 28
Emery, Walter, 77
Enchanting Darkness, An, 126
Encounter, 67
English Instructor, The, 31, 38
English Poetic Diction from Chaucer to Wordsworth, 87
Essays on Modern Quebec Theater, 124
Eugenics and the Welfare State, 131, *131*
Ewing Family Civil War Letters, The, 125, 128
Expedition to Lake Itasca, 90, 115

Faculty Book Award, 104
Fall, Bernard, 59
Fayre Formez of the Pearl Poet, The, 115
Feeding A Billion, 107
Ferris, William G., 107
Fettered Freedom, 6-8, 16
Fifteen Signs before Doomsday, The, 20
Filler, Lewis, 137n.2
Financial Expert, The, 31
Fishel, Wesley, 56, 57, 59, 61
Fisher, John, 34

Foreign Policies of the Founding Fathers,
   64, 88
Forever Afternoon, 121
Formosa: A Study in Chinese History, 63
Foster, E. G., 2
Friends and Neighbors, 57, 58
From Main Street to the Left Bank, 72

Gallagher, Jack, 29, 30, 50-52, 74-75,
   83, 93
Gallin, Bernard, 63-64
Gardner, Martin, 45, 48, 49
Garfinckle, Herbert, 57
Garrity, John, 72
Gilman, Daniel Coit, 1
Gilpin, Alec, 88
Girls, Gangs, Women, and Drugs, 115-16
Glazer, Nathan, 11
Glorying in Tribulation, 126
*Goebbels and National Socialist
   Propaganda,* 37, 38
Going to Washington State, 114
Goldman, Eric, 19
Goodard, W. G., 63
Gordon, Haim, 131
Grain Traders, The, 107
Grassus, Benvenutos, 115
Grateful to Life and Death, 31, 38
"Great Fear," the, 12
Great Lakes Country, 135n.7
Great Railroad Conspiracy, The, 8, 19, *20*
Greeks and Trojans, 28
Greene, Anne, 130
Greene, Graham, 31, 59
Greenhouse Tomatoes, 86
Greer, Thomas, 88
Guide, The, 33

Han Suyin, 67
Hannah, James A., *3*; and the Agency
   for International Development, 71;
   anti-communist stance of, 67; and
   the Civil Rights Commission, 89;
   and Clifton Wharton Jr., 72, 73,

74; educational background of, 1-
   2, 12; and founding of the
   Michigan State University Press, 1,
   4, 5; and Lyle Blair, 26, 74; mem-
   oir of, 8, 83, 84; protection of fac-
   ulty from anti-communist assaults,
   2, 71; resignation of, 71; and
   Russel Nye, 71; shutdown of *State
   News,* 13-14, 71
Hardin, Clifford, 118
Hardin, Edward, 35
Harper, William Rainey, 1
*Harriette Simpson Arnow: Critical Essays
   on Her Work,* 129
Harris, Frank, 28-29, 30
Harvard University Press, 2-4
Head, Beverly, 121
Heist, William, 20, 123
*Henry James and the Naturalistic
   Movement,* 88
Hesseltine, William, 19
Hickey, Dennis, 126
Higginson, Thomas Wentworth, 89
Hildreth, Elom, 59
Hill, Richard, 126
Hirschfield, Charles, 19
Historian, The, 119
History of the Civil Rights Commission, 89
Hoffman, Frederick J., 15, 115
Hofstader, Richard, 19
Hogan, J. Michael, 129
Hogg, Peter, 126
Hohri, William, 111
Homa, S., 86
Howard, Victor, 123
Howarth, Guy, 24
Hunter's Horn, 129, *130*
Huston, Ralph C., 6
Hutchinson, Earl Ofari, 126

I Remember Like Today, 107
Imagine a Woman and Other Tales, 128
In the Service of the Farmer, 83
Indian Legends, 90, 115

International Cooperation
    Administration, the (ICA), 57
"It's Not the Way," 12

Jacobs, Bruce, 121
Jacques Legardeur de Saint-Pierre, 124
Jaffe, Adrian, 87
Johnson, Linda Cooke, 119, *120*
Josyph, Peter, 127-28
Journal of International Marketing, 119
journals, Michigan State University
    Press, 118-20

Kirk, Russell, 13
Korth, Phillip, 107
Kristol, Irving, 67
Kugel, Rebecca, 130
Kuhn, Madison, 38

La Citadelle Enchanteé, 24
LaFarge, Thomas, 114
Lansdale, Edward, 59, 60, 61, 62, 68
Last West, The, 135n.7
Leadership is an Art, 107-8, *108*
"Librarians of Oz, The," 49
Lindholm, Richard, 59
Litton, Ron, 13-14
Lockwood, Y. R., 104
Lodge, Henry Cabot, 34, 58
Loehr, Julie L., 111, 121
Lonely Crowd, The, 11
Lotus Poetry Series, 121-22
Luptowski, Laura, 119

MacPherson, Peter, *122*
Madgett, Naomi Long, 121, *122*
Magic of Persuasion, The, 38
Magsaysay, Ramon, 59, 68
Making of a Myth, The, 64, 88
Malone, Dumas, 2-3, 4
Mansfield and Vietnam, 130
Martin, Robert, 123
Mason, Philip, 90, 115
Mass Communication, 93

Maxwell, Moreau, 63
May, Philip, 5, 14, 33
McCauley, James, 136n.3
McClung, Catherine, 124
McDonel, Clark, 5
McKee, Russell, 14, *15*, 135n.7
McNeil, Donald, 69
McPeek, Gail A., 104, 124
McQuinty, Louis, 63, 64
Mead, David, 19
Medhurst, Martin J., 129
Memoir, 8, 83, *84*
"Memories of Wilde," 29
Merrit, Leroy Charles, 49
Merton, Robert, 116
Michigan American Legion, the, 12
Michigan Folklife Reader, 104, *105*
Michigan Mammals, 85
Michigan State College Bookstore
    Committee, the, 1, 2
Michigan State College Press, the. See
    Michigan State University Press, the
Michigan State University: CIA connec-
    tions of, 57; land grant spirit of, 67;
    Ramparts exposé of, 55-57; and the
    Vietnam project, 56-57, 67
Michigan State University Press, the:
    academic freedom of, 9, 35-38; and
    the Association of American
    University Presses, 10, 77, 78-79,
    117; Board of Directors of, 5, 9, 35-
    36, 72, 97, 118; book design of, 20-
    21, 123; corporate restructuring of,
    118; editorial advisory board of,
    118; financing of, 5, 16-18, 36, 74-
    75, 77, 96, 97, 99; founding of, 1, 2,
    5; high standards of, 6, 8, 9, 51;
    journals of, 118-20; as nonprofit
    corporation, 5, 9, 118; notable
    books of, 85-90; objectives of, 95-96,
    97; as part of Michigan State
    University Libraries, 99; partnership
    with Wayne State University Press,
    84, 104; Program Review

Committee of, 93, 95-97, 100; relationships with university faculty, 50-52, 64; secret subsidization of by government agencies, 57, 58, 59, 65-66, 74, 75, 77; value of an apprenticeship at, 120-21

Michigan State University Press: Guidelines to its History and Objectives, xi, 5-6

Mid-Century Bookclub, 29

Midwestern Progressive Politics, 8, 19, *27*, 108

Miller, Adam David, 121

Mimosa editions, the, 65

Mister Jefferson's Disciple, 20

Morgan, David, 77

Motherwell, Robert, 124

Muelder, Milton, 118

Munn, Clarence "Biggie," 2

Murrow, Edward R., 114-15

My Life and Loves, 29-30

Narayan, R. K., 31, 32, *34*, 68, 70, 136-37n.4

Narrative Journal of Travels through the Northwestern Regions of the United States, 90, 115

Niehoff, Richard, 98

Neville, Howard "Jake," 63, 64, 72

New Essays by Arthur Murphy, 87

Newman, Robert P., 129

Ngo Dinh Diem, 56

Niblock, James, 106

Northeast African Studies, 119

Nuclear Freeze Campaign, The, 129

Nye, Russel, 7; and *A Palace or a Poorhouse*, 83; books by, 6, 8, 43-45, 83; and *Fettered Freedom*, 6-8; and *In the Service of the Farmer*, 83; and John Hannah, 71; and John Hannah memoir, 8, 83; and Lyle Blair, 53; and *State News* shutdown, 13, 71; and *This Almost Chosen People*, 43; and *Two Years Before the Mast*, 65; and *The Wizard of Oz and Who He Was*, 45, 47

O'Brien, Michael, 130

Of Tuning and Temperament, 86-87, *87*

Ojibwa Lodge Stories, 115

Olson, Gregory A., 130

Oscar Wilde: His Life and Confessions, 28-29, *30*

Ottemiller, Francis, 135n.7

"Our Common Tongue," 24

Oxford University Press, 1

Palace or a Poorhouse, A, 83

Payoffs in the Cloakroom, 115

Peoples of Washington, 111

Perrine, Laurence, 89

Perry, Ralph Barton, 3-4

"Petition Respectfully Submitted to President Hannah, A.," 13

Philip Hart: The Conscience of the Senate, 130

Philipson, Morris, 136n.4

Platform for Change, 126

Poetry of the American Civil War, The, 89, 128

Pollack, Charles, 21, 123

Powers, Lyall, 88

Presidential Fellows Program, the, 109

Printer of Malgudi, The, 31

Privatera, Joseph, 34

Process of Kafka's Trial, The, 87

Quadrant, 136n.3

Quest for Corvo, The, 30

Quicksand, 131

Ramparts, exposé of Michigan State University, 55-57, *56*

Read, Herbert, 11

Real Exchange Analysis, 120

"Reconciliation Elegy," 124

Redd, Lawrence N., 85

Reed, Harry, 126

Reeve, Fred, 9

Reisman, David, 11

Renegade Tribe, 111

Repairing America, 111
Rewriting the Good Fight, 123
Rhetoric and Public Affairs, 120
Rhetoric and Public Affairs series, 129, 130
Rhetorical History of the United States, The, 130
Rhinehard, Patricia, 33
Rickover, Hyman, 40
Robinson, Walter S., 60
Rock is Rhythm and Blues, 85
Roll-Hansen, Nils, 131
Rollo, Charles, 34
Roosevelt, Eleanor, 24
Rubenstein, Bruce A., 106, 115
Rural and Urban African Studies, 119
Rutter, William, *10*; and anthologies, 115; and the Association of American University Presses, 10-11; and financing of Michigan State University Press, 16-18; hiring of, 6, 9; later career of, 135n.7; resignation of, 16; and role of the university press, 11, 21-22; and Russell McKee, 14-15; and *State News* shutdown, 13

Sabine, Gordon, 59
Samuel Sewall, 88
Schlesinger Jr., Arthur, 8, 66, 67
Schoolcraft, Henry Rowe, 6, 90
Schools for Democracy, 39, 40
Schossberger, Emily, 34, 42
Schreiber, Isabelle Georges, 24
Schwille, John R., 97
Scigliano, Robert G., 63
Scott, David, 97
Scott, Lawrence P., 126
Selected Works of Henry Lawson, 41
Selzer, Richard, 127, *128*, 128
Seven Deadly Sins, The, 11, 21
Shaw, George Bernard, 29
Shaw, John, 115
Shawn, William, 34
Sheinbaum, Stanley K., 55-56, 57

Sheng Shihts, 65
Sherbo, Arthur, 87
Simon, Lou Anna, *120*
Sinkiang–Pawn or Pivot, 65
Smith, A. J. M., 24, 119
Soils and Land of Michigan, 36
Soviet Penetration of Sinkiang, The, 36
Speaking Through My Skin, 121, *123*
Spender, Stephen, 67
Spiller, Robert, 19
State News, the, shutdown of, 13
Stein, Sol, 29
Steinmetz, Lee, 89
Stetson, Erlene, 126
Stevens, Harry, 19
Stimson, William L., 114
Strandness, T. B., 88
Strauss, Patrick, 88
Student Athlete, The, 85
Studies in the Eighteenth Century Novel, 87
subvention, 117
Suffragists and Democrats, 76-77
Swami and Friends, 31, 136n.4
Symonds, A. J. A., 30

Taking the World in for Repairs, 128
Taylor, Carl S., 108-10, 115, *116*
Television's Impact on American Culture, 42
Test, The, 72
Thant, U, 34
Thirty Years among the Indians, 115
This Almost Chosen People, 8, 43-45
Three Bullets Sealed His Lips, 106, *106*
Tinker, Hugh, 62-63
To Be the Main Leaders of Our People, 130
Trafzer, Clifford E., 111, 130
Tragedy and Paradox of the Fortunate Fall, The, 11
Tragedy of Lyndon Johnson, The, 19
Trials and Triumphs, 128
Trilling, Lionel, 29
Truman, Harry S., 71
Truman and the Hiroshima Cult, 129

Twins of Genius, 8
Two Years Before the Mast, 8, 65, 123

Ulveling, Ralph, 46, 49
Uncertain Self, The, 87
Underwood, Clarence, 85
United States Foreign Relations 1820-1860, 88
United States Information Agency, the (USIA), 57, 58, 68-69
University College, elimination of, 75, 99
university presses: audience of, 80; financing of, 16-17, 79-80; freedom from commercial constraints of, 4, 9, 90; importance of backlist to, 1, 9, 16-17, 101; importance of strong faculty to, 21-22; role in diffusing knowledge, 1; role in prestige enhancement of universities, 9, 80, 87, 89, 95-96
University Publications, 96
University Publishing Associates, 98
Uphaus, Robert, 115

Varg, Paul, 64, 88
Veatch, J. O., 36
Vengeance of the Gods, The, 28
Vickery, Olga W., 115
Vietnam: The First Five Years, 59-63, *60*
Vinall, Jim, 47

Wagner, Linda, 93-94
Waiting for the Mahatma, 31
Wales, John, 39, 40
Walk on the Wild Side, The, 27
Walking North, 121
War of 1812 in the Old Northwest, The, 88
Ward, William, 45
Warner, Rex, 28, 38

Weisinger, Herbert, 11, 88, 119
West, Anthony, 31, *34*
Wharton, Clifton, Jr., 26, 72, *73*, 76, 108-9
What One Man Said to Another, 128
What Roosevelt Thought, 88
White, Sidney, 111
Whiting, Allen, 65
Wickert, Frederick, 59
Wild Life of the Army, The, 89-90, *91*
Wilkinson, Roger, 97, 118
Willard, Hal, 13
William Faulkner–Four Decades of Criticism, 94
William Faulkner: Two Decades of Criticism, 115
Williams, Arnold, 20
Williams, Frederick, 89, 90, 115
Williams, Harry T., 90
Williams, Mentor, 6, 90
Wilson, Robin, 53
Winburn, Newt, 85
Winder, Clarence, 118
Winder, Lee, 98-99
Witter, Sylvan, 107
Wittwer, S. H., 86
Wizard of Oz and Who He Was, The, 8, 45-49, *46*
Womack, William, Sr., 126
Wonderful Art of the Eye, The, 115
Woodford, Frank, 20
World Christ Knew, The, 123, *124*
World is Our Campus, The, 72
Wounded River, 127
Wylie, Kenneth, 126

Yankee Eloquence in the Middle West, 8, 19
Young, Coleman, 127

Ziewacz, Lawrence E., 106, 115